AF225282

Autonomy in Xinjiang:
Han Nationalist Imperatives and Uyghur Discontent

East-West Center

The East-West Center is an internationally recognized education and research organization established by the US Congress in 1960 to strengthen understanding and relations between the United States and the countries of the Asia Pacific. Through its programs of cooperative study, training, seminars, and research, the Center works to promote a stable, peaceful and prosperous Asia Pacific community in which the United States is a leading and valued partner. Funding for the Center comes from the US government, private foundations, individuals, corporations, and a number of Asia Pacific governments.

East-West Center Washington

Established on September 1, 2001, the primary function of the East-West Center Washington is to further the East-West Center mission and the institutional objective of building a peaceful and prosperous Asia Pacific community through substantive programming activities focused on the theme of conflict reduction in the Asia Pacific region and promoting American understanding of and engagement in Asia Pacific affairs.

Policy Studies 11

Autonomy in Xinjiang:
Han Nationalist Imperatives and Uyghur Discontent

Gardner Bovingdon

Copyright © 2004 by the East-West Center Washington

Autonomy in Xinjiang: Han Nationalist Imperatives and Uyghur Discontent
by Gardner Bovingdon

ISBN 1-932728-20-1 (print version)
ISSN 1547-1349 (print version)

Online at: www.eastwestcenterwashington.org/publications/

East-West Center Washington
1819 L Street, NW, Suite 200
Washington, D.C.   20036

Tel: (202) 293-3995
Fax: (202) 293-1402

E-mail: publications@eastwestcenterwashington.org

Website: www.eastwestcenterwashington.org

The *Policy Studies* series contributes to the Center's role as a forum for discussion of key contemporary domestic and international political, economic, and strategic issues affecting Asia. The views expressed are those of the author(s) and not necessarily those of the Center.

This publication is a product of the East-West Center Washington project on *Managing Internal Conflicts in Asia*. For details see pages 69-77.

The project and this publication are supported by a generous grant from the Carnegie Corporation of New York.

Contents

List of Acronyms — v

Executive Summary — vii

Introduction — 1

The Source of Unrest — 3

Uyghur Responses to State Policies — 5

International Factors — 9

Legal Framework for Autonomy — 12

Xinjiang Policy and Practice — 17

Specific Policies and Popular Responses — 23

    The Production and Construction Corps — 26

    Cadre Recruitment — 28

    Culture, literature, history — 30

    Preferential policies — 36

    Pressures for change — 41

Conclusion — 46

Endnotes   49

Bibliography   57

Background of the Xinjiang Conflict   65

Map of the Uyghur Autonomous Region, China   67

Project Information: The Dynamics and Management of Internal Conflicts in Asia   69

    • **Project Purpose and Outline**   71
    • **Project Participants List**   75

Policy Studies: List of Reviewers 2003–04   79

Policy Studies: Previous Publications   80

List of Acronyms

Bingtuan	*see* PCC
CCP	Chinese Communist Party
ETIM	Eastern Turkistan Islamic Movement
ETR	Eastern Turkistan Republic (1944–49)
INA	Ili National Army, the military force of the Eastern Turkistan Republic
KMT	Chinese Nationalist Party under Chiang Kaishek, defeated on the mainland in 1949
MAC	*Minzu* Affairs Commission
Minzu	Official ethnonational category in the PRC; comprises 56 groups, including Uyghurs and Hans
Nationalists	*see* KMT
PCC	Production and Construction Corps
PLA	People's Liberation Army
PRC	People's Republic of China
TIRET	Turkish Islamic Republic of Eastern Turkistan (1933–34)
XUAR	Xinjiang Uyghur Autonomous Region

Executive Summary

This paper analyzes the sources of Uyghur discontent and ethnonational conflict in Xinjiang since the founding of the People's Republic of China in 1949. It argues that the episodes of unrest in Xinjiang have not been simply contemporary manifestations of an enduring culture of violence. Nor have they been the product of foreign intrigues. Instead, while conflict in the region has had several causes, the system of "regional autonomy" operating in Xinjiang must be seen as a principal source of the unrest. Instead of resolving a longstanding political dispute between Uyghurs advocating independence and the Chinese government, this system has deepened Uyghur discontent and exacerbated conflict. To support this thesis, the paper presents both a historical analysis of policy changes over time in Xinjiang and a close study of current policies in the region.

Autonomy arrangements around the world have been enacted to protect both states' territorial integrity and the fragile rights of minorities. But all autonomy regimes privilege territorial integrity over absolute responsiveness to the demands of the autonomous group: they are a compromise between (a) states, which want unabridged sovereignty and homogeneous populations; and (b) peoples that want self-determination, generally meaning independence. Thus we should not be surprised to find both state actors and autonomous groups pressing for renegotiation of their agreements. Yet there are dramatic differences in the degree to which states have honored their formal commitments and in the amount of pressure for change brought to bear by nominally self-ruling groups. In Xinjiang, the political system has chronically thwarted Uyghurs' exercise of self-rule and thus provoked and exacerbated Uyghur discontent.

One demonstration of the absence of regional autonomy in Xinjiang is that extreme policy swings there tightly followed those in the rest of China and its other autonomous provinces. Relatively tolerant policies in the early 1950s were replaced by strongly repressive and assimilationist ones as the country embarked on the Great Leap Forward in 1958. A return to moderation in the early 1960s was then reversed again with the advent of the Cultural Revolution in 1966. By the end of that movement in 1976, pressures to assimilate linguistically and culturally, the persecution of religious practices and personnel, and attacks on respected authorities had profoundly alienated most Uyghurs. Deng Xiaoping's announcement of economic reforms in China in 1978 was soon followed by somewhat more tolerant cultural and economic policies in Xinjiang, though signally without relaxation of political controls. After public demonstrations in Xinjiang in1988 and 1989 and a violent uprising in 1990, Deng ordered a crackdown in that province. The political clampdown in Xinjiang was accompanied by new restrictions on culture and religion that have remained in place up to the present.

Both long-standing and recent policies by leaders in Beijing and Ürümci have combined to deepen discontent among Uyghurs, and the official refusal to allow open expression of dissatisfaction in the region has only increased that discontent. Invariably harsh responses to demonstrations have left the field of overt political action to the violent and desperate while failing to address the concerns of the majority. The multifaceted repression of religion—including the closure of mosques, supervision and dismissal of clerics, and the prevention of religious practice by the young—has made Islam in Xinjiang more rather than less political in the Reform era. And while Beijing has decentralized economic authority during the Reform era, it still wields considerable economic influence in Xinjiang, abetted by the region's disproportionate concentration of state enterprises and dependence on subsidies. The pattern of economic development in Xinjiang has ensured the further stratification of the labor market, a stratification that is often blamed for strengthening oppositional identities and aggravating intergroup friction around the world. The mining and export of Xinjiang's oil and gas according to Beijing's dictates and by an almost entirely Han Chinese workforce has increased Uyghurs' sense of exploitation. Heavy Han immigration into the region and the consistent choice of Han officials for the top positions at all levels of Xinjiang's party bureaucracy strike many Uyghurs as colonial practices. Finally, both Han immigration and state policies have dramatically increased the pressure on Uyghurs to assimilate linguistically and culturally, seemingly contradicting the explicit protections of the constitution. This pressure has deepened the popular perception of a gulf between Uyghurs and Hans.

To suggest that Chinese policies in Xinjiang have been a key source of conflict is to imply that more moderate policies would have provided a better outcome. Historical counterfactuals are notoriously shaky ground for comparison. Furthermore, the frequency of ethnic conflict and violence in Xinjiang during the Republican era might have led us to expect both to continue after 1949. The argument here is not that ideal policies would have eliminated discontent and friction entirely. Instead, this paper contends that, had the CCP hewed more closely to what international legal scholars describe as the minimal principles of autonomy, Xinjiang would have seen less conflict. It also argues that the particular departures of Chinese practice from that minimal model exacerbated regional conflict in specific ways.

There is considerable disagreement on how conflict might be reduced in Xinjiang. Many Uyghurs and foreign observers assert that rigid policies and crackdowns on dissent have precipitated the protests and violent episodes of recent years. In contrast, Chinese officials and scholars claim that the lax PRC policies of the 1980s allowed separatist organizations and Islamic extremists to grow in number in the region and become more influential. Careful attention to the modern political history of Xinjiang demonstrates that the former view is more plausible. Organized protest and violence emerged in the region long before the 1980s. Furthermore, dissatisfaction since then has not been confined to Islamists and separatists advocating violence; ordinary Uyghurs have expressed profound discontent with Chinese rule in Xinjiang.

Beijing's policies could have been moderated, and they can still be ameliorated now. Sadly, however, the September 11 attacks have eliminated Chinese leaders' incentives to enact moderate policies. The announcement of the global "war on terror" appears to have emboldened Beijing to respond to dissent by tightening its grip on the region, and thus to diminish further the small amount of autonomy Uyghurs and others currently exercise. Chinese policy advisors have recommended precisely this recourse. But further reduction in the scope of autonomy in Xinjiang is avoidable and certain to exacerbate discontent.

Autonomy in Xinjiang: Han Nationalist Imperatives and Uyghur Discontent

The modern political history of the region today known as Xinjiang has been tumultuous and often violent. But the renewed spate of public protests and deadly clashes in the region over the last quarter century are not simply contemporary manifestations of an enduring culture of violence. Nor, as some Chinese scholars and officials have argued, have they been the product of foreign intrigues. Instead, while several factors have contributed to the conflict, Xinjiang's very political structure must be seen as one root cause of the unrest. The full name of the region's territorial unit, the Xinjiang Uyghur Autonomous Region, suggests that Uyghurs—the largest non-Han population in Xinjiang—largely govern themselves. In fact, the system officially touted as providing autonomy in Xinjiang enacts heteronomy, or rule by others. This paper makes the case that Xinjiang's political system has exacerbated the region's conflict and deepened Uyghur discontent.[1]

The promise of autonomy arrangements has always resided in their potential to protect both states' territorial integrity and the fragile rights of resident minorities. Statesmen and scholars have proposed autonomy either to avoid discord or to resolve it. Indeed, a major study of "minorities at risk" advocates autonomy as the sole solution acceptable to all sides in otherwise insoluble conflicts between governments and their minority populations (Gurr 1993). Socialist states were among the first to adopt institutions of formal autonomy, and many claimed thereby to have "solved their national question" (Connor 1984: xvi).

In reality, however, all autonomy regimes privilege territorial integrity over absolute responsiveness to the demands of the autonomous group: they are a compromise between; (a) states, which want unabridged sovereignty and homogeneous populations; and (b) peoples that want self-determination, generally meaning independence. Such compromises often leave neither side satisfied. Thus we should not be surprised to find both state actors and autonomous groups pressing for renegotiation of their agreements. Yet there are dramatic differences worldwide in the degree to which states have honored their formal commitments and in the amount of pressure for change brought to bear by nominally self-ruling groups. A foundational text on the law of autonomy regimes observes that "autonomy is understood to refer to independence of action on the internal or domestic level" (Hannum and Lillich 1980: 860). The definition ill fits the system of governance in Xinjiang. As subsequent sections of this study will show, Beijing has allowed Uyghurs almost no independence of action.[2] The party-state has actively and premeditatedly thwarted the emergence of a political elite in Xinjiang capable of pressing for Uyghur collective interests, and it has similarly squelched ordinary Uyghurs' attempts to respond to or influence policies in Xinjiang. For those silenced voices, Beijing has substituted an official line that most Uyghurs are quite satisfied with the way Xinjiang is ruled.

The defects in Xinjiang's politics and governance are related to larger systemic problems in Chinese politics. The PRC remains a single-party state and continues to prevent various groups from articulating demands and from organizing to pursue their interests. Beijing still employs propaganda, silences dissent, punishes transgressions with violence, and extirpates independent political organizations throughout the country. All of these practices are amplified in the political system in Xinjiang. While desperate not to lose any territory, Chinese leaders attribute particular strategic significance to Xinjiang as both a source of oil and gas and a conduit for still more energy from Central Asia—energy they feel is crucial to China's continued economic growth. Concern about ethnic conflict and fear that many Uyghurs aspire to independence has made party officials in Xinjiang much more sensitive to and often more brutal in suppressing perceived challenges than their counterparts elsewhere. The lodging of so much power in the hands of Han Chinese officials has only increased the fractiousness of the region.

The Source of Unrest: The Grievances of Many, Not the Organization of a Few

But to charge that China's autonomous regions, prefectures, and counties do not enjoy the self-rule Beijing claims is not particularly controversial. Indeed, an early observer derided the system as "regional detention,"[3] and many scholars have argued that the PRC's system of "*minzu* regional autonomy" provides little actual political autonomy (Dreyer 1976; Heberer 1989; Mackerras 1994).[4] Several analysts have made this argument with specific reference to Xinjiang (McMillen 1979; Moneyhon 2002; Stein 2003), and two scholars have even suggested that, instead of providing autonomy, Xinjiang's administration is "colonial" (Bachman 2004; Gladney 1998). This paper attempts to move beyond such formal critiques to causal analysis, showing how the political system's specific features and problems have led to particular forms of Uyghur discontent and resistance.

It might be argued that, while instability in Xinjiang is the product of the system of autonomy, that instability has little to do with Uyghur grievances. For instance, Svante Cornell (2002) claims on the basis of comparative study that systems of autonomy can themselves cause conflict rather than resolve it. In many cases, these systems even facilitate the emergence of secessionist movements. Cornell draws on the substantial literature (Brubaker 1996; Roeder 1991) in arguing that the Soviet Union's federal system of national republics contributed to the disintegration of that state. But he argues that these authors have been wrong to ignore institutions below the republic level. Cornell finds that, in subrepublican autonomous units as in the republics, the institutionalization and fostering of distinct identities increase autonomous groups' "cohesion and *willingness* to act"; the institutions themselves, he further argues, enhance the "*capacity* of [groups] to act."

In general, a state establishing an autonomous region formally acknowledges the territorial boundaries of that region and the identity of the group or groups exercising autonomy. The state further allots resources to help protect the distinct identity of the titular group. In so doing, the state both strengthens group solidarity and sanctions a territorial frame for that group's political aspirations. The state also usually allows the establishment of distinct political institutions, the cultivation of leaders to run those institutions, and the local control of media and educational organs. Together, Cornell argues, these institutions increase rather than reduce the likelihood of conflict and therefore of secession. Cornell adds that a state's recognition of an autonomous group may increase that group's international visibility and thus raise the probability of international intervention in any resultant conflict (Cornell 2002: 251–56).

Three factors Cornell identifies have been of undoubted importance in Xinjiang politics. First, formalizing the boundaries of Xinjiang and naming it the "Xinjiang Uyghur Autonomous Region" without doubt gave a convenient frame to Uyghur political imaginings (Bovingdon 2002b). Second, institutionalizing *minzu* identities and assigning privileges on the basis of those identities strengthened them considerably.[5] Finally, these practices have given greater international prominence to Uyghur discontent—though only, it must be added, as violent protests rocked the region in the 1990s. Judging from the number of formal governmental inquiries and international academic conferences on Uyghurs and Xinjiang over the last decade, the region and people claim more attention than any others in China except Tibet and the Tibetans.

Yet while Cornell's argument is formally compelling, it cannot explain the vastly different outcomes in China's various autonomous regions. The PRC's other provincial-level autonomous regions—Mongolia, Guangxi, Ningxia, and even Tibet in the 1990s—have been far quieter than Xinjiang.[6] Nor does his model capture well the system actually operating in Xinjiang. Most of the features Cornell considers standard in systems of autonomy are absent (or present only in truncated form) in that region.

> *The PRC's other provincial-level autonomous regions...have been far quieter than Xinjiang*

Xinjiang's government institutions have been heavily colonized by Hans, and have been subordinated at all levels to the heavily Han party structure. Uyghur (and other non-Han) leaders have been carefully chosen and forced to act as apologists and even boosters for unpopular policies, all but ensuring that these leaders would develop no popular constituency. Media and educational institutions have remained under tight state control in all periods except the 1980s. Indeed, it can be argued that political controls on these institutions are tighter than they were at the beginning of the reform era. Thus, while Chinese policies in Xinjiang might be credited with strengthening Uyghurs' sense of collective identity, those policies have if anything reduced Uyghur's capacity to act collectively.

In sum, a purely systemic argument cannot fully account for the unrest in Xinjiang. The region's institutions of autonomy have indeed contributed in various ways to the conflict, but we cannot fully understand that contribution without considering long-standing Uyghur grievances. Departure from the system of *minzu* regional autonomy in Xinjiang—such as the manipulation of authority, violent policy swings, and state actions never codified in (or limited by) law have also provoked Uyghur discontent.

Uyghur Responses to State Policies

Before the Chinese Communist Party (CCP) took full control of China in 1949, many Uyghurs expected that they would soon enjoy full political independence in Xinjiang. Indeed, they had been told as much by Mao over a decade earlier (Connor 1984), and Xinjiang's last governor under the Nationalists (KMT), Zhang Zhizhong, had speculated publicly about the region's eventual "decolonization" following the examples of India and the Philippines (Benson 1990; Bovingdon 2001). Yet after the founding of the People's Republic, CCP officials asked Uyghurs to be satisfied with autonomy, described as "control over their own affairs."

Those Uyghurs who accommodated themselves to this lesser promise hoped to reverse the legacy of the past few decades under Han rule. In the Republican era (1911–49), Han officials had governed Xinjiang at the provincial and several subprovincial levels. During this period, Uyghurs had faced discrimination in employment and political appointments. At the same time, officials had invited Hans to settle Xinjiang and had shown them various kinds of favoritism, in some cases even providing them choice farmland by forcibly evicting Uyghurs. Chinese officials arrogantly expected Uyghurs to adopt the culture and language of Hans if they wanted to succeed, though they also doubted the ability of most to do so. And Uyghurs faced economic exploitation by greedy officials and sharp-dealing Han and Hui (Chinese-speaking Muslim) merchants. Exorbitant taxes, rampant corruption, and high prices for imported goods left many Uyghurs and the region as a whole mired in poverty.[7]

Given the CCP's prerevolutionary promises, Uyghurs and other locals might well have expected autonomy to include government by Uyghurs and other Turkic Muslims, the regulation of the economy to benefit the region and its inhabitants, control over cultural and linguistic matters, and freedom to practice their religion. And from 1949 to 1958, many Uyghurs were pleased with progress on these fronts. But after that period, conditions in Xinjiang began to deteriorate with the advent of several major policy shifts. Though Uyghurs, Qazaqs, and others gained positions in government, Han Party Secretaries would continue to dominate the region's political decisionmaking. Pressures for residents to assimilate culturally and linguistically, which had been much reduced immediately after 1949, reached unprecedented levels in 1958 and continued more or less until 1977. Initial tolerance of religious practice turned into naked persecution during the same period. Uyghurs also confronted unprecedented ideological pressures from party cadres and teachers, and they watched in further dismay as Han immigration to the region shot up dramatically. In addition, from 1964 on Xinjiang was the site of China's nuclear testing program. In the judgment of many Uyghurs interviewed decades later, the system that emerged combined some of the worst features of the Republican regime with unexpected and unwanted new ones.

Not surprisingly, growing dissatisfaction in Xinjiang emerged in various forms. Though a series of violent events in Xinjiang since 1990 have received international press coverage, these incidents have been rare in comparison to those in Palestine, Chechnya, Aceh, or Mindanao. The apparently long periods of relative calm and representations of the region's politics by the Chinese government might lead us to believe Uyghurs have been largely content. In fact, however, we now know that Xinjiang has seen more episodes of collective and violent action from the founding of the PRC to the present than were previously reported. We now have a fuller record of the frequency and depth of the region's internal conflict, thanks in part to the work of foreign journalists, scholars, and Uyghur activists. Beijing has also recently permitted publication since the late 1990s of much more information about the conflict; this flow has increased following the September 11 attacks, after PRC officials judged that highlighting the Xinjiang conflict might help justify the government's hardline policies toward Uyghurs and significantly increase Beijing's credentials in the "war on terror."

Officials and scholars working for the state have consistently claimed that the episodes of regional strife were and are the work of a small handful of extremists opposed by most Uyghurs. Yet the major episodes of violent or collective action have revealed popular discontent with Chinese policies in Xinjiang. The depth and spread of this dissatisfaction have been visible in the size of protest crowds and in the way episodes of protest have snowballed quickly (and in many cases apparently spontaneously) despite Beijing's best efforts to prevent the formation of nonstate organizations. The protests and riots also indicate the specific roots of the discontent. The slogans shouted or written on placards and banners at these mass gatherings provide strong evidence that the particulars of the system of autonomy have provoked Uyghurs and exacerbated conflict.

the major episodes of violent or collective action have revealed popular discontent with Chinese policies in Xinjiang

Many demonstrations have revealed unhappiness with Han rule and immigration. In 1981, for instance, after the trial of a Han youth accused of killing a Uyghur in a fight, a major riot broke out in the streets of Kashgar. Participants vocally denounced Hans and the Han government and called for a "Republic of Uyghurstan." Though the number taking part is not known, Chinese sources note that the riot gripped the whole city for a period, and hundreds were injured. Four years later, the dismissal of a popular Uyghur governor provoked another major demonstration: In December 1985, Ismayil Ähmäd was removed from his post as chairman of the Xinjiang government and "kicked upstairs" to Beijing to head the *Minzu* Affairs Commission (*Minwei*). As the news of Ähmäd's dismissal spread, Uyghur students at Xinjiang University boycotted classes, and several thousand marched in the streets of Ürümci to denounce the move, protesting that Ähmäd had been cashiered for insisting that all Uyghurs receive employment before more Hans were allowed to immigrate. Slogans at the demonstration included "Hans out of Xinjiang" and "Independence, Freedom, and Sovereignty for Xinjiang." Uyghur students in Beijing staged a similar protest 10 days later. A decade later, over three days in April 1995, there was a spate of protests in northwest Xinjiang. Participants advocated the end of Communist control in the region and independent states for Qazaqs and Uyghurs. There are reports that at least 50,000 people participated in these protests, and that 100,000 took part in strikes on the final day. And during the widely publicized Ghulja (Yining) demonstrations in early February 1997, over one thousand protestors yelled that they would expel Hans and that they wanted nothing to do with the Chinese government (Dillon 2004: 60, 68–69, 97; Rudelson 1997: 133; Toops 1992: 86–87)

A number of protests in Xinjiang have targeted policies governing religion and the treatment of Muslims. Students in major demonstrations in both 1988 and 1989 protested the publication of books they believed disparaged Uyghurs, Qazaqs, and Islam; they also demanded more general respect for their culture and religion. In Khotan in 1995, hundreds took part in a riot after the dismissal by Han authorities of a popular Muslim cleric accused of delivering subversive sermons. During the 1997 Ghulja uprising, protestors marching behind a banner printed with the Islamic *shahada* announced defiantly they would brave prison for the right to advocate their religion openly, and there were calls to "establish an Islamic caliphate" (Dillon 2004: 60, 70, 96).

Protestors have also claimed on several occasions that official policies have abridged Uyghurs' rights or failed to eliminate discrimination. In the 1985 Ürümci demonstration described above, students also protested Beijing's rumored intention to extend China's one-child policy to non-Hans, and criticized the "expropriation" of Xinjiang's mineral resources. In December 1988, Uyghur students in Beijing demanded genuine equality and the protection of *minzu* human rights (Dillon 2004: 60; Xu Yuqi 1999: 112).

The use of Xinjiang's barren southeastern Lop Nor region for nuclear weapons testing also incensed many Uyghurs. In November 1985, Uyghur students in Beijing demonstrated to protest against nuclear tests. Some 1,000 people also converged on the Lop Nor test site in 1993 and demanded the tests end. PLA soldiers fired on the protestors, and fighting broke out; in the melee, some participants entered the compound and damaged vehicles and equipment (Dillon 2004: 60, 155).

Finally, in at least one event, demonstrators raised all of the issues mentioned above. The Baren uprising in April 1990 began with a protest in a mosque against family planning, weapons testing, and oil exploitation before turning into a violent riot with calls for "jihad" and the overthrow of communism (Bovingdon n.d.; Dillon 2004: 62–65).

Skeptics might object to this emphasis on the overt demands of protestors in Xinjiang and, indeed, on the protests themselves. First, protest messages might be strategic, trumpeting some issues as covers for others. (Two of the most consequential pro-democracy demonstrations in PRC history—those in 1976 and 1989—began as memorials to recently deceased leaders.) Furthermore, popular demonstrations in Xinjiang have been infrequent and generally small affairs compared to those in "hot spots" in Southeast Asia or the Middle East. Yet as many scholars have pointed out, limiting our attention to open expressions of discontent under drastically repressive states may lead us to grossly underestimate the depth and scope of that discontent.[8] Behind the mainly placid facade of Xinjiang politics, a number of scholars have uncovered substantial evidence of everyday resistance in the form of sub rosa complaints and private noncompliance (Bovingdon 2002a; see also Dautcher 2000; Rudelson 1997; and Smith 2000). One reason to have confidence that the rare public articulations of discontent express widespread popular sentiment is that they overlap substantially with these private expressions. Officials in Beijing and Ürümci have dismissed the public protests as the work of a small number of malcontents, yet the combined record of overt and covert resistance suggests rather that the majority of Uyghurs are unhappy with the system of autonomy and the course of politics.[9] Nor can the protestors be considered mere dupes of foreign powers, as Chinese officials have claimed.

International Factors

International factors have affected Xinjiang politics in at least three ways. First, the Soviet Union provided a model (and mirror) for Chinese policies. Second, several states have intervened in Xinjiang. Third, multinational interventions in the 1990s to protect human rights around the world led Uyghurs to hope they would find allies in their struggle. Yet these international factors have not been the root cause of unrest and conflict in Xinjiang.

The Soviet Union was above all a model, both positive and negative, for Chinese planners in the country's peripheral regions. CCP officials consistently shaped the system of *minzu* regional autonomy and conducted their policies with one eye on Soviet precedents. These officials read Lenin and Stalin and cited chapter and verse from the texts of these leaders to justify their management of the "*minzu* question." As had Moscow, these officials chose to institutionalize and protect distinct identities and enact territorial rather than merely cultural autonomy. Their use of preferential policies to cultivate cadres and recruit students from among non-Han populations also followed the Soviet example. Even the harsh clampdowns on "local nationalism" and ruthless purges of titular officials—alongside periodic openings—could have been taken directly from the Soviet playbook, which included Stalin's crackdown in the 1930s, Khruschev's "thaw" in 1956–57, and renewed restrictions in the 1960s.

At the same time, Chinese officials sometimes departed from the Soviet model with the rationale that it did not fit China's circumstances, as in the choice of a unitary rather than federal state. On occasion, these officials chose radically different policies out of ideological disagreement, as with the 1958 Great Leap Forward. Finally, Chinese policymakers and their advisors watched the Soviet Union especially closely during the tumultuous Gorbachev era and the period of disintegration. They have unquestionably studied the Soviet example to avoid precipitating the crises that faced Moscow. One irony is that, while many foreign analysts had long predicted on cultural and religious grounds that Central Asia would be the source of the Soviet Union's eventual demise, the Central Asian republics were among the last to leave the union (Roeder 1991).

Several foreign governments have sought to influence politics in Xinjiang, with the United States and the Soviet Union mounting the most consistent efforts. In the late 1940s, as the Communists appeared increasingly certain to defeat the Nationalists, the United States sent agents to Xinjiang and Tibet to collect intelligence and conduct rearguard harassment (Laird 2002; Shichor 2004). In the 1960s, the American government supported Uyghur language broadcasts beamed into China by Radio Free Europe. Broadcasters included Erkin Alptekin, son of the most prominent Uyghur independence activist Isa Yusuf Alptekin. Though Washington agreed to stop the Uyghur service as a favor to Beijing after their rapprochement in the 1970s, this move did not end American intervention. In yet another apparent turnabout, Congress established Radio Free Asia (RFA) in 1996, again projecting a signal into China among other states. The station's Uyghur service, begun in 1998, broadcasts information critical of the Chinese state and maintains a call-in line Uyghurs use to complain of mistreatment (Gladney 2004: 385). Though Beijing routinely blocks RFA, many Uyghurs are reported to listen to and have taken inspiration from the station.

For its part, the Soviet Union had begun to send advisors and intelligence officers to Xinjiang no later than the 1930s. Even after the CCP's victory in 1949, Moscow certainly sought to maintain political and commercial influence in the region. Soviet officials also took an active part in the 1962 exodus of 60,000 disaffected Uyghurs and Qazaqs from Xinjiang across the border, distributing prepared exit papers and assuring refugees that living conditions in the Soviet Union were far superior to those in Xinjiang. In addition, as the Sino-Soviet split deepened, Moscow authorized daily Uyghur-language broadcasts from a station in Tashkent. According to a Chinese source, the station broadcast messages that Uyghurs deserved self-determination, that their homeland was "East Turkistan," and that if they voluntarily joined the Soviet Union they could have their own federal republic. Moscow also initiated border incursions into Xinjiang in 1969 and appeared to be preparing for further strikes, though the Sino-American détente likely quashed the plan.[10] Two decades later, Moscow also unintentionally influenced politics in Xinjiang by dismantling the Soviet Union. There is little doubt that the emergence of independent Central Asian states named for various Turkic groups gave new inspiration to Uyghurs hoping for political change.

Transnational organizations have also inspired the Uyghur cause. Uyghurs established formal political organizations in Kazakhstan and Kyrgyzstan soon after independence. These groups sent various magazines, books, and cassettes into Xinjiang and sought greater international prominence for the independence movement. (While these organizations still exist, they have received heavy pressure from their host governments at Beijing's behest since the establishment of the Shanghai Cooperation Organization in 1996.) Similar groups operate around the world. The oldest Uyghur political organizations, founded by Isa Alptekin, still operate in Turkey, although Beijing has achieved modest success in inducing Istanbul to rein them in. Some wealthy Uyghurs in Saudi Arabia have also provided support and funds to advocates of independence and political Islam. Europe, Australia, and North America have Uyghur organizations as well. Though PRC leaders have attempted to persuade the international community that some of these groups contain terrorists, with one exception (discussed in the next paragraph) they have not succeeded. But while these organizations have given Uyghurs greater international visibility, there is scanty evidence that they have influenced politics in Xinjiang, despite some leaders' boasts and Beijing's accusations.[11]

Of far greater significance than transnational organizations for Xinjiang politics have been a series of high-profile multilateral interventions in the 1990s (Bosnia, Kosovo) that seemed to indicate human rights now trumped sovereignty in the international arena. The 1999 NATO intervention in Kosovo reportedly greatly inspired Uyghurs and simultaneously rang an alarm bell for China's leaders. If NATO was willing to attack a sovereign European state to protect a Muslim minority, many Uyghurs hoped (and Beijing feared) that the international community might well do the same for Uyghurs and Tibetans in China (Lawrence 2000; Ma Dazheng 2003: 106–22). Yet September 11 and the subsequent "war on terror" greatly reduced the likelihood of international intervention on Uyghurs' behalf. The declaration by the United States and the United Nations in the summer of 2002 that the previously little-known Eastern Turkistan Islamic Movement (ETIM) was a terrorist organization deeply gratified Beijing and simultaneously led many Uyghurs to despair of receiving international support. State-controlled media in Beijing and Ürümci used ambiguous language to suggest that the United States had condemned all advocates of an "Eastern Turkistan" as terrorists.[12]

PRC officials have also claimed that transnational organizations concerned about Uyghur self-determination are tools of imperialism or servants of plots to split up China.[13] But Uyghur discontent cannot be attributed solely or even principally to international factors. Of far greater importance have been the origins, legal institutions, and actual implementation of Xinjiang's autonomy regime.

> *Uyghur discontent cannot be attributed solely or even principally to international factors*

Legal Framework for Autonomy

Origins

In contrast to many other cases around the world, but similar to that in Aceh and Papua in Indonesia, the system of autonomy established by the CCP in Xinjiang, as in China's other peripheral regions, was imposed upon titular groups rather than negotiated with them. Materials published decades later show that, from 1949 through 1954, Uyghur leaders pressed Mao and other leaders for a literal interpretation of Lenin's doctrine of self-determination. At a 1951 conference in Ghulja, the former seat of government of the Eastern Turkistan Republic (of which more below), a group of Uyghur leaders proposed the establishment of a "Republic of Uyghurstan" with the capacity to regulate all its internal affairs. Xinjiang CCP officials—on instructions from Beijing—hastily convened a meeting to condemn the proposal and ensure that this "incorrect idea" not spread widely (Zhu Peimin 2000: 335). Yet the idea did not disappear. A speech by Zhou Enlai at a 1957 conference in Qingdao, released only in 1980, shows Beijing was aware many Uyghurs continued to hope for a federal system and self-determination. At different points in that speech, Zhou told assembled officials that China "could not" establish and "had no need" to establish a federal system on the Soviet model (Zhou Enlai 1980 (1957)).[14] By the late 1980s, party theorists would claim that the system of *minzu* regional autonomy "completely…fit China's situation" (Zhang Erju 1988). They could not, however, claim that it suited Uyghurs.

Institutions

The Xinjiang Uyghur Autonomous Region (XUAR) was established with great fanfare in October 1955. While in principle Uyghurs thereby received title to the property,[15] what they confronted was in fact a condominium of nested autonomies, leaving them a patchwork of territories—principally Qumul and Turpan, Aksu, Kashgar, and Hoten districts—divided and surrounded by the others. This parcelization of the territory had taken place in a series of steps over the previous eighteen months, and presented Uyghurs with a *fait accompli* at the time of establishment of the XUAR. It has recently come to light that Xinjiang party officials had proposed in 1953 to set up autonomies "from the top down," but the Central Committee in Beijing decreed that the order instead proceed from "small to large" (Wang Shuanqian 1999: 249).

The division of Xinjiang into a number of smaller autonomies was a stroke of administrative genius. In parcelling out "sub-autonomies," the CCP simultaneously satisfied the goals of embodying the idea that Xinjiang belonged to 13 different *minzu* and of counterbalancing the overwhelming political and demographic weight of Uyghurs.[16] The political and material interests of each of the other constituted groups were therefore to a certain extent aligned with the central government and against Uyghurs. By the end of 1954, more than 50 percent of the province's area had been allotted to autonomous townships, districts, counties, and prefectures.[17] In 15 out of 27 units thus established, the titular *minzu* constituted less than 50 percent of the population; in Tacheng and Emin county autonomous districts, the titular *minzu* (Daghuor and Mongol) made up, respectively, less than 17 percent and 12 percent of the population. A portion of today's Bayinguoleng was made a Mongol autonomous prefecture, although Mongols constituted only 35 percent of the prefectural population; in 1960, after the government annexed to it an "almost purely" Uyghur region, it came to occupy one third of Xinjiang's area

> *The division of Xinjiang into a number of smaller autonomies was a stroke of administrative genius*

(Atwood 2004: 39).[18] In a study on *minzu* relations in Xinjiang, government analysts Mao Yongfu[19] and Li Ling observed not long ago that

> Qirghiz, Tajik, and other *minzu,* despite the small size of their populations, nevertheless have autonomous prefectures and counties belonging to their own *minzu;* in those areas, they belong to the self-governing *minzu.* By contrast, in [those places] Uyghurs have once again [sic] become non-self-governing *minzu*…This is something we must look into diligently (Yin Zhuguang and Mao Yongfu 1996: 173).

The authors' apparent surprise at this situation was rather disingenuous; the autonomies' order of establishment demonstrates this had been precisely the intention forty years before.[20] But the question persists: In what sense are the various *minzu* "self-governing"?

Every official account of "minzu regional autonomy" (*minzu quyu zizhi*) makes liberal use of the expression "masters of their own house" (*dang jia zuo zhu*). The system of autonomies, advocated by theorists and enacted by the Chinese Communist Party (CCP) since 1949, supposedly gave non-Hans mastery of their regions. In Xinjiang, the purpose of this system, far from making non-Hans head of their house, has been simply to keep them in the house. The granting of Uyghur influence over affairs in the Xinjiang Uyghur Autonomous Region (XUAR) has taken a back seat to the consolidation of CCP control and the crushing of any movements that advocate independence, or even the more modest goal of "real autonomy."

Though maintaining publicly that power stems from the people, the party leadership has always taken pains to extend authority only from the top down, giving no quarter to power organized locally. Party leaders have also considered Uyghurs politically untrustworthy, allotting them very little power. It has selected and promoted officials who exercise power only in a fashion consonant with CCP goals, and reserved the decisive authority at virtually all levels for trusted Hans imported from posts in China proper.[21] The legal framework of autonomy has exacerbated this disenfranchisement.

The legal framework of autonomy has exacerbated this disenfranchisement

Constitutional Provisions

Successive PRC constitutions and associated organic laws have codified a national plan for *minzu* regional autonomy within (a) a set of institutions and cultural and linguistic rights that these institutions were intended to secure, and (b) a carefully specified relationship between those institutions and the central government. Xinjiang's distinctive features and political history notwithstanding, its "autonomous" government institutions emerged from that national plan and therefore strongly resemble those in China's other autonomous regions.

Both the 1952 "Program for Implementing *Minzu* Regional Autonomy" (hereafter "Program") and the national constitution of 1954 made clear the expectation that autonomous units at county, prefectural, and provincial levels would have governmental organs broadly similar to those at the corresponding levels in China proper. Stipulated elements included the standard branches of government, a People's Congress with elected representatives chosen from the titular group or groups but also including Hans, and obedience to higher level government organs.[22] Both documents provided that actual institutional forms could be determined by the wishes of the "great majority of the people and leading figures with links to the people" of the titular group or groups.[23] Military organization was not left to local discretion. Though the Program allowed for the establishment of local police cadres, all security personnel including soldiers fell under the "unified national military system." Between 1950 and 1955, troops in the predominantly Uyghur and Qazaq Ili National Army (INA), formerly the military arm of the Eastern Turkistan Republic, were folded into the PLA or demobilized and settled on paramilitary farms. In both cases, these troops fell under direct CCP control (McMillen 1979: 53; Shichor 2004: 127–29, 132).

The first constitution also committed the government to drawing up a national autonomy law; though the Government Administration Council had passed the Program in 1952, a formal law would be promulgated only in 1984 and then amended in 2001. In addition to the organizational principles above, the 1984 Autonomy Law affirmed in general terms what had been practices of long duration in the autonomous regions: "affirmative action" in the recruitment of college students, the hiring of employees at state enterprises, and the training of base-level government cadres.

The articles of the Autonomy Law reveal the limitations built into the system.[24] Article 15 indicates that all autonomous government organs are under the leadership of the State Council, and all must "obey the state council." Article 20 grants organs of autonomy the right to "alter or suspend" policies or orders promulgated by higher-level government units, yet makes such actions subject to approval by those superior units. And while it acknowledges the right of autonomous regional governments to draw up locally appropriate "statutes on autonomy and specific regulations," Article 19 also grants the National People's Congress the authority to approve or reject such statutes.[25]

Having studied the original law and its 2001 revision, Chinese legal scholar Yu Xingzhong concludes that the political system it specifies "certainly does not correspond to what is usually understood [by] the term 'autonomy'" (Yu Xingzhong n.d.).[26] Studies of the system with special reference to Xinjiang reach much the same conclusion (Moneyhon 2002; Sautman 1999; Stein 2003). One author argues that, whatever rights the state constitution and autonomy law grant in principle to local decision-making bodies, national laws "take most of those rights away" by requiring that central government organs approve all local decisions. Indeed, Moneyhon finds that the system of governance established in Xinjiang fails to satisfy any of five criteria proposed by international legal scholars as fundamental to autonomy. In a widely cited article, Hannum and Lillich argue that legal autonomy required, at minimum, an independent local legislature not subject to central veto power, a locally chosen executive, an independent judiciary, local decisionmaking not compromised by the center's "reservation…of general discretionary powers," and binding power-sharing arrangements (Hannum and Lillich 1980: 886–87). Moneyhon observes that Beijing retains veto power over the decisions of Xinjiang's People's Congress. The center has chosen each of Xinjiang's successive executives, and the supreme court retains supervisory power over Xinjiang's courts. Furthermore, Beijing reserves broad discretionary power over Xinjiang's affairs, including how autonomy is implemented; and the center unilaterally allocates power over resource exploitation, policing, and other matters unbound by power-sharing arrangements (Moneyhon 2002: 137, 142–44).[27] Though the PRC system has dramatically departed from the Soviet model in many particulars, on this last point it clearly follows Moscow's example. In its relations with its union republics prior to 1991, Moscow "both define[d] the sphere of authority and exercise[d] it" (Gleason 1990: 65).

Yet as confining as this political legal framework proved for Uyghurs in Xinjiang, actual political practice has made still greater incursions into the region's hypothetical autonomy. In Yu Xingzhong's estimation, rather than providing a new legal framework for the system, both the 1984 and the 2001 versions of the Autonomy Law simply recorded in statutory form some features of established practice. Legal revisions have followed policy changes, not vice versa. Yu argues that the Chinese government "is still relying on policy rather than law to regulate its affairs" (Yu Xingzhong n.d.). A full account of the workings of *minzu* regional autonomy in Xinjiang must therefore include not only structural limitations of the system but also a brief history of political developments and actual political practice.

actual political practice has made still greater incursions into the region's hypothetical autonomy

The following two sections, the first covering policy trends in Xinjiang since 1949 and the second analyzing particular policy areas in greater detail, develop the argument that the actual workings of the system contributed to regional conflict rather than resolving it. The first section traces the evolution of Communist Party rule over Xinjiang and the Uyghurs since 1949. It demonstrates that Xinjiang, far from being autonomous, was almost entirely at the mercy of the major political conflagrations in China proper. The second section characterizes policies in Xinjiang governing population, the settlement of Hans on paramilitary farms, cadre recruitment, culture, religion, affirmative action, and economics. The section lends substance to the claim that political actions by Beijing and Ürümci operated specifically to deny Uyghurs and others control over local affairs.

Xinjiang Policy and Practice

Chronology, 1949–2000

Limited space prevents the recounting of political events in Xinjiang prior to 1949. Two features of the social climate of the Republican Era (1911–49) must be noted, however, as they figured prominently in Communist Party leaders' calculations of strategy.[28] Anti-Han sentiment was deep and widespread among Uyghurs, partly as a consequence of decades of harsh, exploitative rule by Han warlords and local officials. At the same time, general antipathy to Hans, which might have drawn Uyghurs and other Turkic peoples (principally Qazaq, Kyrgyz, and Tajik) together, was counterbalanced by religious, political, and cultural differences of long duration.

general antipathy to Hans…was counterbalanced by religious, political, and cultural differences of long duration

Turkic peoples had cooperated several times in the 20th century to establish independent governments—for example, in (a) the Turkish Islamic Republic of Eastern Turkistan (TIRET) of 1933–34, controlling the southern third of the region from Kashgar; and (b) the Eastern Turkistan Republic (ETR) of 1944–49, governing the northwest from Ghulja. In the Ili National Army (INA), the military force raised by the ETR, Uyghurs, Qazaqs, and members of other groups fought side by side. Yet those governments covered only small parts of the vast territory of what is today Xinjiang, and fell apart as much from internal disagreements as from external attacks. Resentment of Hans posed a challenge to CCP strategists, but antagonisms within the Turkic population provided the party an opportunity to pit groups against one another and thus to manage that challenge in postrevolutionary governance.

Following the "peaceful liberation" of Xinjiang by the PLA in 1949, regional army head Wang Zhen demobilized thousands of soldiers and redeployed them on a network of paramilitary farms (subsequently named the Production and Construction Corps, or PCC) throughout the province.[29] Having installed a tractable government leadership headed by the Tatar Burhan Shähidi and the Uyghur Säypidin (Saifudin) Äzizi, Wang and other party officials set about establishing strategies for managing non-Han groups.

In the early 1950s, those strategies were relatively tolerant. The CCP's *tongyi zhanxian* ("united front") policy counseled the establishment of links with "progressive members" of social and religious elites, which in turn required minimal interference with business, religious practice, or social norms. The party did, however, gradually take control over religious institutions through the China Islamic Association, as well as through the confiscation of mosque lands and the forcible replacement of religious courts with "People's Courts" (McMillen 1979: 113–14).

By the mid-1950s, as Mao pressed regional leaders to make more sweeping economic changes throughout the country in the so-called "socialist tide," the Xinjiang leadership faced resistance to such initiatives. Collectivization required antagonizing the "progressive elites" with which the party had previously cooperated; and, as would happen many more times, the attempt to mobilize the exploited classes (mostly peasants, in the overwhelmingly agrarian region) against the elites instead drove many Uyghurs and others together against the party. In China proper, Mao invited criticism of CCP policies from the masses in the 1956 Hundred

Flowers campaign. The vehemence and volume of protest shocked the leadership, which then unleashed the Anti-Rightist movement in 1957 to silence the opposition. In Xinjiang, Uyghurs, Qazaqs, and others denounced the system of autonomy as a sham and demanded a far greater role in local governance. Party hardliners swiftly inflected the Anti-Rightist movement into an "Anti-local nationalist" movement, accusing such critics of seeking to "rule Xinjiang as an independent country" or resist CCP rule.[30] Officials found particularly irksome the charge that the PCC soldier-farmers were "Han colonialists." Faced with such challenges, the party redoubled its efforts to mobilize class against *minzu* interest (Dreyer 1976: 150–57; McMillen 1979: 116, 117).

Mao's radical voluntarist Great Leap Forward, begun in 1958, led in Xinjiang to calls for a rapid cultural homogenization to accompany and facilitate the Leap. This movement naturally meant greatly reduced official tolerance for difference. Ethnicity itself became an "obstacle to progress." Party leaders stepped up attacks on Islam and other "backward customs" (Dreyer 1976: 157–63; McMillen 1979: 118). As is now widely known, the combination of Great Leap policies, bad weather, and the central government's ill-chosen decision to export grain to meet its debts to the Soviet Union brought on a terrible famine. Party leaders temporarily prevailed on Mao to restore a more moderate economic course, producing a Thermidor in the early 1960s. Cultural policies in Xinjiang relaxed modestly in the period, as officials acknowledged linguistic and cultural differences would persist over the long term. Talk of speedy assimilation subsided.

Party leaders stepped up attacks on Islam and other "backward customs"

Yet despite policy retrenchment, widespread starvation in the interior of China intensified the Great Leap's impact on Xinjiang. In addition to party-mandated population flows, vast numbers of hungry migrants poured into Xinjiang on their own initiative. This population "surplus" flow drove Han immigration into the region to over 800,000 in both 1959 and 1960, its highest levels ever (Hannum and Xie 1998: 324). PCC farms welcomed many of the refugees to settle and claim land, provoking increased resentment by Uyghurs and others. As noted earlier, over 60,000 Uyghurs and Qazaqs fled across the border in 1962 into the Soviet Union, prodded by exasperation with CCP policies and lured by radio propaganda. The deepening Sino-Soviet split played a role in this exodus: Soviet consular officials had apparently connived in the mass migration by distributing previously prepared travel papers. For officials in Xinjiang and Beijing, the sheer numbers of emigrants raised the frightening prospect of hostile former citizens receiving military training, then assisting in the cause of "Soviet social imperialism" by helping to take Xinjiang by force. In response, the government sealed the border and forcibly relocated thousands of non-Han families away from the border zone, replacing them with Han PCC members (Dreyer 1976: 169–70; McMillen 1979: 120–23).[31]

Minzu policies changed course again in the mid-1960s, as renewed radicalization at the highest level of the party led to the Cultural Revolution (1966–76). Officials appointed to the Cultural Revolutionary Small Group, which replaced the XUAR Party Committee for several years, and the initially mostly Han Red Guards raised demands for cultural conformity to a new extreme. While Red Guards in China's heartland collected and destroyed artifacts of the past, in Xinjiang (as in Tibet and other non-Han regions) they targeted non-Han culture. Difference once again became a sign of backwardness. Activists frightened the various Turkic peoples into shedding their habitual clothes, adornments, scarves, and hats for Mao suits. They destroyed mosques and even forced many religious leaders and ordinary Muslims to raise pigs, apparently in an attempt to engineer rapid and thorough assimilation.[32]

The punishments Cultural Revolutionaries visited on intellectuals betrayed particular truculence toward Uyghur culture: the famous linguist Ibrahim Mutte'i was tortured by having the huge volumes of a multilingual dictionary he had helped edit (with full CCP support at the time) dropped on his head.[33] Ordinary citizens were not exempt. Residents who had lived through the period described witnessing men being subjected to shaving in the streets, for even beards were interpreted as signs of defiance. A Qazaq woman raising a towheaded Uyghur boy dyed his hair black and shaved his eyebrows to avoid persecution. Uyghurs meeting each other in the street learned to initiate every greeting with "Long live Chairman Mao" in Chinese.[34]

In retrospect, it is clear that policies toward non-Hans were at their most assimilationist and intolerant during the Cultural Revolution. After Mao's death in 1976 and the fall of the Gang of Four, party leaders faced a crisis. The Cultural Revolution had alienated a large segment of the population throughout China. Yet resentment was particularly grave among

Uyghurs and other non-Hans: for them, it had been not merely a political and social assault, but an attack on their identities. The continuation of hardline policies seemed certain to provoke increasing discontent and thus instability. But more tolerant policies allowing cultural exploration and freer religious practice, might similarly open the door to unrest. Nagged by these concerns, Chinese policymakers charted a zigzagging but narrowing course between openness and control.

Chinese policymakers charted a zigzagging but narrowing course between openness and control

In 1980, Hu Yaobang, one of the younger leaders in the Central Committee and soon to be promoted to CCP Secretary General, traveled to Tibet to investigate local conditions. Appalled by the poverty and despair he found there, Hu urged that hardline policies toward non-Hans be relaxed. To remedy Tibet's situation he advocated "genuine autonomy," economic initiatives appropriate to local conditions, renewed cultural and scientific projects, and the gradual transfer of Han officials back to China proper. He made similar proposals for Xinjiang in July 1980.[35] Hu felt at the time that Xinjiang presented less of a separatist threat than Tibet because it lacked exiled religious or political leaders like the Dalai Lama and had no "overseas support" for independence (Dillon 2004: 36). The XUAR Party Committee speedily adopted Hu's suggestion and announced in August 1980 over the objections of hardliners that large numbers of Han cadres would be transferred out of Xinjiang.

Held responsible for the increasing student and popular demonstrations which had convulsed Beijing and other major cities in 1986, Hu Yaobang was purged in 1987. Former Xinjiang Military Commander Wang Zhen, who had fought openly with Hu over his proposed changes, then ordered that the more accommodating policies toward Xinjiang be scrapped. A Han official siding with Wang is reported to have said "You give [Uyghurs] autonomy and they will only turn around and create an East Turkistan." The official was disgusted with the proposal to send Hans back to the interior, and insisted that only "hard-liners like Wang Zhen" could keep Xinjiang stable.[36] An official report produced for internal circulation a few years later concurred in this view. The dismissal of Han cadres had "made it impossible," the report argued, "for Han cadres to work in Xinjiang with a sense of security, and it also sowed serious ideological chaos among minority *minzu* cadres. [It] was extremely harmful to *minzu* solidarity" (Zhang Yuxi 1993: 358).

Deng Xiaoping's economic reforms had brought unprecedented prosperity to China's interior over the previous decade. The conservative leadership of Xinjiang initially sought to block the local implementation of reforms, fearing that they would destabilize the region. To many, the pace of the reforms that did come was frustratingly slow. People would continue to joke wryly in the mid-1990s that, while the interior had wholeheartedly embraced capitalism, socialism was still being pursued (if not realized) in Xinjiang. Nevertheless, by 1992, the XUAR leadership had come to an agreement that reform was inevitable. The popular Uyghur official Ismayil Ähmäd announced the same year that the central government would cede more autonomy to Xinjiang. He suggested this would include local authority over foreign trade, control of the border, and administration. At least one analyst saw this move as an attempt to counter the appeal of separatists in the wake of the Soviet Union's collapse (Cheung Po-ling 1992).

But the party complemented the loosening of economic policy with political tightening, a combination that has continued up to the present.[37] There have been two central components of that tightening. Yearly *yan da* ("Strike Hard") campaigns, as with their counterparts in the interior, aim to capture large numbers of suspected criminals in massive dragnets and then prosecute them on an accelerated schedule. As in China proper, these campaigns target violent property crimes, drug rings, and the like; in Xinjiang, however, they also focus on political crimes.[38] Second, Public Security personnel have arranged periodic sweeps (*zonghe zhili*, or "comprehensive management") to shore up control in each locality.[39] A number of my Uyghur informants received orders from their work units to take part in these sweeps in 1997, as the party fretted about the return of Hong Kong to Chinese rule. One ardently anticommunist man told me he was simply notified a week in advance that he would be traveling to the south to spend two months praising CCP policies. He was to go from house to house within "suspect" villages, chaperoned by two Hans, patiently correcting people's misconceptions and erroneous political views. It was, he observed, like being forced to eat a steaming plateful of pork. Another informant related being forced more regularly to take short propaganda trips to areas around Ürümci. Interviews with a third revealed that the strategy did not involve surveillance and propaganda alone. A doctor, she was dispatched for several months with only a few days' notification to several poor rural areas to treat patients and to pass on the party line while doing so.[40]

The party, concerned after the breakup of the Soviet Union that Uyghurs in the newly independent states might have greater latitude for political activism, complemented its domestic clampdown with an international offensive. After helping found the "Shanghai Five" group in 1996 (consisting of China, Russia, Kazakhstan, Kyrgystan, and Tajikistan, later joined by Uzbekistan in 2001), Beijing pressured the other members of the group to crack down on Uyghur separatists active within their territories. In exchange, China pledged massive loans and aid to the member states and gave vocal support to their actions against their own internal challengers. China has since successfully demanded the extradition of suspected separatists from many of the member states as well as Pakistan and Nepal, despite protests from international organizations.[41]

The September 11 attacks provided an unprecedented opportunity for the Chinese government to defend its policies in Xinjiang. Where previously Uyghur dissidents had been described as "splittists," they were now branded as "violent terrorists," and government press releases depicted the battle with Uyghur separatists a part of the global "war on terror."[42] Though the Chinese government explicitly denies it, recent reportage and fieldwork strongly suggests that political controls in Xinjiang have grown more stringent since the end of 2001.[43]

To understand those political controls and their recent trajectory, we turn now to specific policy areas. The following section characterizes policies governing immigration and family planning, the PCC, cadre recruitment, culture, religion, and economics, with attention to Uyghur responses to those policies.

Specific Policies and Popular Responses

Population

One of the party's most effective tactics for counteracting political pressure from Uyghurs has been, in effect, to import a loyal Han constituency. Government-sponsored immigration of Hans into the region has been a central component of CCP policy in Xinjiang. It has also provided compelling evidence that officials in Beijing and Ürümci felt they could never hope to persuade the majority of Uyghurs to be satisfied with their political status in China.[44] Soon after the PRC's founding, the State Council prepared a plan to transfer some two million citizens from China's interior. The target was extraordinarily ambitious, in terms both of mobilizing Han migrants and of finding places for them in a largely arid region. Yet officials overfulfilled the plan. Between 1950 and 1978, the party cajoled, induced, or ordered roughly 3 million Hans to move to Xinjiang (Qiu Yuanyao 1994: 223–40; Wang 1998: 37–38). Many settled on PCC farms, and in the early years PCC cadres traveled to major population centers to recruit more volunteers directly (McMillen 1979: 61). Massive and sustained immigration increased the Han proportion of the population from roughly 5 percent in 1949 to over 40 percent in 1978. But while moving Hans into Xinjiang was relatively easy in the pre-1978 period, making them stay after that time became increasingly difficult.

The first major disturbances in Xinjiang during the reform era involved not Uyghurs but Hans agitating to return to the interior. Many Han youths had been "rusticated" (*xiafang*) from Shanghai and other major urban centers during the Cultural Revolution. Some had already returned home clandestinely, discovering to their dismay that local authorities refused to find them jobs or housing. Their residence permits had been permanently transferred to Xinjiang. In February 1979, Han youths unwilling to return to Xinjiang and other "remote" areas rioted in Shanghai. In late 1980, several thousand Shanghainese youths who had been sent to Aksu demonstrated to protest both local conditions and the government's refusal to allow them to return to Shanghai. The party responded by dispatching former regional military leader Wang Zhen to stifle the disturbance, "requesting" that local units improve conditions for young Han settlers and increase propaganda that stressed how important the youths were to countering Soviet designs on the region. Yet despite Wang's efforts, emigrants would top immigrants for the first time in 1981 (McMillen 1984: 574–76).[45] Increasingly desperate at the upsurge in violence and continued Han flight, Beijing recalled Wang Zhen's old comrade Wang Enmao from retirement to serve once again as Xinjiang's First Party Secretary. The latter proposed a compromise to keep the bulk of the former Shanghai youths in Xinjiang: A small number judged to have "qualifications" would be allowed to return to Shanghai, while the majority, though required to remain in Xinjiang, would be permitted to have one child resettled in Shanghai by the state (Zhu Peimin 2000: 356).

Despite the efforts of the two Wangs, authorities failed to induce a net inflow of Hans into Xinjiang again until 1990, when a new wave of immigrants moved to Xinjiang by choice rather than under compulsion. This inflow resulted from the combination of market forces and the declining significance of the national household registration system (*hukou*), which had been established in the 1950s precisely to stanch migration.[46] Deng Xiaoping's economic reforms had enabled farmers to lease land, individuals to strike out in private business, and underemployed rural and urban workers to seek jobs in new enterprises. Both geography and central policies initially favored the coastal regions, but by the early 1990s, the government had announced favorable land lease rates and tax abatements in China's western hinterlands—the so-called "West-leaning" policies—to lure labor and capital to the west. Finally, burgeoning markets in food, land, and labor greatly diminished the power of the household registration system to fix people in one place. By the late 1990s, the combined effects of these policy changes were plain to see in the thousands of simply dressed, heavily burdened people pouring out of the Ürümci train station each day, drawn by rumors of land and jobs in the "great Northwest."

The party's latest concern has been the scarcity of the most desirable kinds of immigrants to Xinjiang: educated youths; technical workers; and committed, politically reliable cadres. It has tried a variety of stratagems to remedy those deficiencies, including subsidies to college graduates willing to immigrate and temporary "swaps" of cadres from the interior with groups in Xinjiang. Perhaps most strikingly, the party announced quietly in April 2000 that it was reassigning 100 demobilized army officers from China proper to head local CCP branches responsible for "political, legal, military, and recruitment affairs."[47] There is no doubt that officials in Beijing expect the recently launched *Xibu da kaifa* ("Go West") initiative—which will funnel vast resources into infrastructural development in Xinjiang and other western provinces—to attract Han immigrants of all types in large numbers. By means of the rail spur to Kashgar, completed in 1999, the initiative is also expected to bring a demographic transformation to southern Xinjiang, which has remained overwhelmingly Uyghur despite the decades of prior immigration. Though the government can no longer order Hans to immigrate, at least one prominent official has renewed the practice of recruitment trips to the interior. In a 2004 interview published in one of China's top nationally distributed newspapers, Xinjiang First Party Secretary Wang Lequan observed pointedly during an inspection tour of Shanghai that Xinjiang was short on "qualified personnel" and its workers were of "poor overall quality." The interview ended with his plea for "talented people of all types" to immigrate to Xinjiang and serve as cadres, managers, or technicians.[48]

Many Uyghurs have consistently opposed state-sponsored Han colonization as an abridgement of their hypothetical autonomy. Even before the founding of the XUAR, Uyghur leaders and intellectuals warned the influx of Hans would diminish their political influence and force cultural assimilation. In the reform era, Uyghurs worried immigration would drive them out of jobs, a concern only compounded by the extension of national family planning policies to non-Hans in Xinjiang in 1988. Since then, urban Uyghurs have been formally limited to two children, and those in the countryside to three, with some exceptions.[49] Uyghurs resent this policy for at least three reasons. First, many consider CCP-mandated birth restrictions proof of colonialism—a decision made by an alien power that they would never have made. In their view, no category of social life more clearly constitutes "their own affairs" than do fertility decisions, which therefore fall under the purview of autonomous rights. Second, many Uyghurs object on religious grounds that in controlling births, the state is arrogating to itself a power it has no right to wield. Third, an overwhelming number of Uyghurs feel that, had millions of Hans not immigrated to Xinjiang, the region would not now be facing population problems.[50]

Many Uyghurs have consistently opposed state-sponsored Han colonization as an abridgement of their hypothetical autonomy

The Production and Construction Corps

Officials in Beijing and Ürümci have deployed many of those Han immigrants in a manner that neatly complemented the division of Xinjiang into subregional autonomies. Redeployment of demobilized Nationalist, INA, and Red Army soldiers into the PCC (or *bingtuan*) at strategic points throughout the region enacted a subtler parcelization of the territory.[51] PCC units that were set up along the margins of "troubled" regions, along key transport arteries, and around hubs provided the potential to control travel and isolate Xinjiang's subregions with very modest manpower. Heavy concentrations of PCC farms in Kashgar, Aksu, and Qumul districts were also intended to counterbalance the overwhelmingly Uyghur population in those areas. Though the *bingtuan* was initially billed as a force to protect Chinese sovereignty in sensitive border regions, the pattern of deployment of its units makes plain that defense against foreign invasions was never the planners' primary worry. The concern of first importance was and would continue to be Uyghur agitation for an independent Xinjiang. The complexion of the PCC underscores this point: it has been overwhelmingly Han since its establishment. A recent publication praises the *bingtuan* not only for quelling the 1990 Baren uprising and similar disturbances but for "preventing over 8,600 people from leaving" during the mass exodus of Qazaqs and Uyghurs in 1962 (Yang Zhenhua 1997: 15).

It is a supreme irony that the PCC boasts more of the trappings of autonomy than any other entity in Xinjiang: according to an official scholar, it "administers its own internal affairs," claiming its own Public Security apparatus, courts, procuratorate, judiciary, and jails. It is answerable only to Beijing, not to the local party organization or government of Xinjiang (Zhu Peimin 2000: 423, 422).

The organization's demographic significance in Xinjiang is unmistakable. In 1974 *bingtuan* members reached 2.26 million in number, or one-fifth of the total population and two-fifths of the Han population in Xinjiang. The organization was disbanded in 1975 but reconstituted six years later on the strong advice of former head Wang Zhen following several episodes of interethnic violence. Twenty years later, it had almost returned to its former size, claiming 2.22 million members, of which 88.3 percent (1.96 million) were Han—35 percent of Xinjiang's total Han population in 1994.[52] Officials and scholars have lately increased calls to expand the organization still further. Uttering a sentiment widely shared among Hans but seldom articulated in public, one scholar recently wrote bluntly that "Hans are the most reliable force for stability in Xinjiang."[53] His text, intended for policymakers, provided a detailed plan for further Han colonization: He argued, for instance, that PCC sites near Qumul must be strengthened to enable full control of the passage from Xinjiang to the interior, and that those near Kashgar should be beefed up to isolate Xinjiang from turbulence in Central Asia. Further deployments, he said, should "draw a circle" around southern Xinjiang by filling in "blank spaces"—one between Aksu and Korla, and another between Hotan and Ruoqiang. The expansion of PCC organizations in the latter region, this scholar remarked brightly, "will prove an excellent conduit for changing the *minzu* population ratio in Hotan, which has gotten out of balance" (Ma Dazheng 2003: 123, 234–35).

Both the system of nested autonomies and the network of strategically located PCC farms have given non-Uyghurs in Xinjiang a stake in the current system. It goes without saying that logistical and military factors decisively favor the PLA. The strategic deployment of immigrants and local governments in the region has ensured that, were Uyghurs to join together in a peaceful demand for independence tomorrow, they would be opposed not only by the over 7 million Hans, but by another 2 million members of other Turkic, Xibo, and Mongol groups.

The party has further incorporated the non-dominant groups into the current system through targeted recruitment that mirrors and reinforces the effects of the territorial parcelization. By insisting on a sort of Noah's ark principle, in which each political organ must have token members of all or most of the 13 "indigenous" *minzu*, the system dilutes the already meager influence of Uyghurs and gives other groups disproportionate authority in the system.

Cadre Recruitment

The Communist Party has also successfully co-opted many Uyghurs, as it has members of the smaller groups. Through careful selection, training, and promotion of loyal Uyghur cadres, the CCP has added substantial numbers to the government without compromising its policymaking autonomy. Uyghurs in regional and local government are frequently called upon to announce the party's unpopular policies, all but guaranteeing those officials will not develop a local power base and blunting the criticism that Hans alone rule the region.[54] The recruitment has followed a consistent pattern.

Uyghurs and other non-Hans were best represented at the lowest levels of government. By mid-1961, over 85 percent of county magistrates and deputy magistrates were non-Han;[55] over half of the commissioners and deputies at district, prefectural, and regional levels were non-Han. Yet according to McMillen, "the key departments and organs of Xinjiang administration…largely remained in the hands of Han CCP members…." In October 1965, non-Han cadres comprised 106,000 (55.8 percent) of the total cadre population of 190,000. The continued (though reduced) preponderance of non-Hans was again tempered by a skewing toward the bottom: fewer than 10 percent of non-Han cadres were leaders at the county level or above (McMillen 1979: 48).[56] Furthermore, the ratio dropped dramatically during the Cultural Revolution. Over 99,000 of the 106,000 non-Han cadres received damning political "labels" and were dismissed from their positions between 1966 and 1976.

Deng Xiaoping's reforms, and in particular the policies advocated by Hu Yaobang, reversed this trend. By the end of 1983, nearly 100,000 non-Hans, now considered to have been "wrongly labeled," had been reinstated as cadres. In combination with the quickened training and selection of minority *minzu* stipulated by Hu, the reinstatement brought the number of non-Han cadres up to 181,860 (or 43.1 percent), a substantial increase. On the other hand, the non-Han percentage of Xinjiang cadres remained over ten points lower than it had been in 1965 ("XUAR *gaikuang*" bianxiezu 1985: 52–54).[57]

While showcasing long series of figures on non-Hans at various levels of government, books vaunting the system of self-government delicately sidestep the key indicator of political authority: Party secretaryships. As McMillen put it, in the Mao era "every government organ and enterprise from the regional level down" had a party official, "normally a Han," who exercised real control (McMillen 1979: 48). Another observer notes dryly that there was "never… any suggestion that Party leaders in the nationality areas would need to be members of the relevant nationality" (Mackerras 1994: 156). This pattern has not changed appreciably: More than two decades into the reform period, non-Han party committee heads are still exceedingly scarce.

Indeed, the percentage of non-Han rank-and-file party members in Xinjiang has remained far below population proportions. In 1987, only 38.4 percent of party members in Xinjiang were non-Han, though non-Hans comprised over 60 percent of the population. These numbers have subsequently fallen: in 1994, the percentage of non-Han party members had decreased to 36.7 percent.[58] Despite the calls for "nativization" of government ranks in autonomous regions, there has never been a corresponding initiative in the party. Säypidin had warned in 1957 that proposing "nativization" of the party was "counter-revolutionary." Decades later, the official justification for eschewing targeted recruitment is that party members have no particularist loyalties and are therefore capable of representing all groups without prejudice. To call for *minzu* quotas in the party would therefore be "unscientific" (Guo Zhengli 1992: 92).

Uyghurs have long been acutely aware of recruitment policies. For years, the class of several dozen Han students learning Uyghur at university (among the lowest scorers on college entrance exams, and most of them reluctant in their major) have been sent to a Uyghur area in the countryside for an annual Practicum, to build language skills and learn at first hand about living conditions. Musing on this phenomenon in 1997, one rural cadre said ironically that "in the future these people will be leaders and [Party] secretaries," so local governments must always take pains with the Practicum arrangements.[59]

Uyghurs are thus quite underrepresented in the government apparatus, particularly at the higher levels, and severely underrepresented in the party. Recruitment policies have in a sense dovetailed neatly with the policy on immigration. Over time the increasing numbers of Hans have made it easier to justify Han predominance in government.

In interviews, Hans invariably approved of the recruitment patterns while Uyghurs willing to discuss the matter strongly objected.[60] Even those not themselves implicated in the Han-Uyghur rivalry felt the system was skewed toward Hans. A Xibo man who had once announced proudly to me he suffered no discrimination because "no one knows I'm not Han" admitted one day that he had lost patience with official propaganda contrasting equal opportunity in China to discrimination in the United States:

> Our media say the U.S. discriminates, but even so, a black man can
> become head of the Defense Department. Of Commerce. Of the
> Supreme Court [sic]. In China, does the Supreme Court have a single
> *minzu?* Does the Military Affairs Commission in Beijing? Damn![61]

Such comments are not to be found in Xinjiang newspapers or other media. Indeed, the same system which has placed Han party officials in charge of non-Hans at all levels of government has, with the exception of a brief period in the 1980s, prevented the open articulation of grievances about that fact.

Culture, literature, history

On consolidating his authority in 1978, Deng Xiaoping had announced a new era by calling for new openness to intellectual exploration. In China's interior, this call elicited a wide variety of cultural products, from "scar literature" to cinema to Democracy Wall postings.[62] In Xinjiang, Uyghur authors began to write novels, essays, and poetry. Themes that had previously been forbidden and perspectives that would have been harshly punished only a few years ago, now were cautiously being published. Writers in the several oases penned works exploring the past and conjuring a politicized collective identity (Rudelson 1997). The revered author Abdurehim Ötkür wrote poems and allegorical political novels. Historian and poet Uyghur Turghun Almas produced a number of historical articles and books claiming (often rather creatively) that Uyghurs had a long history as a nation and had established many independent states. Officials initially tolerated these heterodox writings, either from inattention or out of confidence in Deng's wisdom.

Yet as with other *minzu* policies, this tolerance changed after the student protests of the 1980s were followed by the 1990 Baren uprising. A huge rally in Ürümci in 1991 criticized Almas and unnamed others for fanning the flames of Uyghur separatism. Officials announced tighter controls over publications. The staffs of several presses were shaken up (as with the Kashgar Youth Press) or replaced wholesale (as with the editorial board of the journal *Kashgar Literature*). Since that time, censors have read submissions to Uyghur journals with increased scrutiny; a code indicating the sub-editor responsible for each article is affixed to the bottom for quick reference. Novel manuscripts face a gauntlet of censors before publication, and even approved novels have faced difficulties. Zordun Sabir's *Ana Yurt* (*"Motherland"*), a three-volume dramatization of the Eastern Turkistan Republic (1944–49) that was published after several rounds of revisions demanded by censors, was later banned anyway for fear it would revive hopes for Uyghur independence.[63] Perhaps concerned that previous book bans had only driven up prices and whetted reader's appetites for forbidden text (Bovingdon and Nabijan Tursun 2004), officials chose to turn the ban into violent theater. In 2002, they staged a public book burning to extirpate lingering copies of forbidden works by Turghun Almas and others.[64]

Audio tapes of poetry or music, extraordinarily popular among Uyghurs in the reform era, also face increasingly strict scrutiny. Those rare allegorical works with hidden or ambiguous messages that have passed the censors (along with works to which listeners attributed meanings not originally intended by their authors) have often circulated widely, only to be banned for having "unhealthy social effects." Such was the fate of a collection of Abdurehim Ötkür's poems, previously published legally but released as dramatic recordings after his death in 1995, and of another long poem titled <u>Dehqan bolmaq täs</u> ("It's hard to be a peasant"). A number of famous Uyghur musicians have produced tapes with songs they were later forbidden to be performed in public (Forney 2002; Smith forthcoming).

Unfortunately, officials in the reform era have returned to past practices in dealing harshly with outspoken individuals. During the Mao era, Abdurehim Ötkür, Turghun Almas, Ibrahim Mutte'i, and many other intellectuals spent considerable time in jail for expressing unpopular views, as had political figures condemned as "local nationalists" in 1957. Since the late 1980s, participants in major demonstrations and people suspected of harboring "separatist" ideas (very broadly defined) have been sent to jail for varying periods, often without formal charge.

the limits placed on Uyghur cultural production have convinced many that the party will not allow them to speak freely

In sum, the limits placed on Uyghur cultural production have convinced many that the party will not allow them to speak freely. They therefore conclude that the party has much to hide. In an atmosphere of fear and mistrust, readers and listeners attribute extra weight to the subtlest signs of dissent.[65] This is one reason religious belief and practice, long opposed on ideological grounds by the party, provokes such passion in Xinjiang.

Religion

Religious faith and piety for Uyghurs are as politically sensitive as the matter of cadre recruitment and as culturally significant as restrictions on public expression. The journal of the Xinjiang Academy of Social Sciences, widely read by policymakers, recently described the challenge officials believed they faced: one scholar wrote that, for those *minzu* for which religious belief is essentially coextensive with group identity, "the believing masses consider attitudes toward their religion to be attitudes toward them" (Liu Zhongkang 1996: 67).

While government control of religion has noticeably relaxed in many areas of the PRC—among the Dai in Yunnan, the Hui in the north and southwest, and even to some extent in Tibet—the same cannot be said for Xinjiang over the last decade.[66] To be sure, the party did loosen control of religion in the early 1980s as part of its overture to Uyghurs and others after the antireligious excesses of the Cultural Revolution. One obvious sign was the great number of mosques rebuilt. In Kashgar District in southern Xinjiang, for instance, there had been 5,500 mosques (107 in Kashgar City alone) before the Cultural Revolution began in 1966. These figures had already declined considerably from their levels in 1949.[67] The decline had been the consequence, noted a "religious investigation team" dispatched from the Xinjiang Academy of Social Science, of "greatly elevated consciousness of the masses," though the team's report also allowed that quite a few mosques had been taken over by communes during the collectivization movement in 1958.

One indication of the devastation of the Cultural Revolution can be seen in the further reduction in the numbers of mosques in Kashgar District during that period. Only 392 usable mosques remained by the 1970s; only two mosques stayed open in Kashgar City. Muslims responded vigorously to Deng's broadening of cultural policies. In just 1980 and 1981, communities reclaimed or rebuilt over two-thirds of the original operating before 1966, so that by the end of the latter year there were 4,700 mosques in Kashgar District and 93 in Kashgar City (Zongjiao yanjiusuo Yisilanjiao diaocha zu 1983: 21–23). Mosque construction continued in the district throughout the 1980s. Many villages had increased resources as a consequence of the agricultural reforms of the early Deng era, and the communities decided to build mosques with the new wealth.

But the April 1990 Baren incident caught officialdom by complete surprise. In addition to the violence of the uprising and its evident popular support, what stunned party leaders most was the news that participants had claimed openly that Islam would conquer Marxism-Leninism (Liu Zhongkang 1990: 50). In the aftermath of Baren and in response to the shocking collapse of the Soviet Union, the government reversed its previous policy of tolerance. Officials prosecuted "illegal religious activities"—defrocking suspect clerics, breaking up unauthorized scripture schools (mädräsä), and halting the construction of mosques. In 1991, 10 percent of roughly 25,000 clerics examined by officials were stripped of their positions (Harris 1993: 120–21). The party instituted new regular political examinations for Imams, decreeing that only those judged patriotic and politically sound could continue to serve. Those restrictions, along with the stipulation that all new clerics be trained at Xinjiang's sole religious institute in Ürümci, have continued to the present. After a decade of turning a blind eye to mosque building, officials felt construction had exceeded acceptable limits. In 1990, cadres in Akto County (where Baren is located) closed 50 mosques judged to be "superfluous" and cancelled the construction of 100 more out of fear that religion was getting out of control (Dillon 2004: 73).

Yet despite the crackdown, propagandists in Kashgar continued to complain of "indiscrimate (*lan*) construction of mosques" five years later: by 1995, the Kashgar District had approximately 9,600 mosques, more than twice the number in 1981 and "already plenty enough to satisfy the needs of normal religious practice by the believing masses."[68] Certain religious personnel, officials warned, engaged in wanton building with the excuse that the number of religious sites was inadequate. Even worse, some clerics reportedly established schools and classes Qur'an study without official permission, or "took on talip."[69] There were reportedly more than 4,000 talip in the district in 1995 (Kashi diwei xuanchuan bu 1995: 37). This explosion in religious interest ran directly counter to party plans.

Every version of the PRC constitution has maintained, and textbooks on religious policy repeat, that all of China's citizens have two freedoms with respect to religious belief: the freedom to believe, and the freedom not to believe. Yet officials have worried for years that continued religious belief in Xinjiang threatens party authority and, worse, that it might provide a breeding ground for Uyghur political mobilization. The government's chosen strategy, therefore, has been to protect the freedom of people not to believe, while endeavoring to "dilute religious consciousness" in the population (Yin Zhuguang and Mao Yongfu 1996: 233). The principal aim of official policy in securing both freedoms is to make religion a *sishi* ("personal matter"). Over the long term, this policy is intended to end the social and intergenerational transmission of religiosity. Interrupting that transmission in turn serves the larger project of reducing the distinct (and oppositional) identities of Uyghurs and other Turkic Muslims.

The party has placed special emphasis on eliminating the pull of religion on two groups: party members and students. This drive has been a matter of growing urgency. Since 1978, substantial numbers of Uyghur and other Muslim party officials have become religiously observant. Though the constitution guarantees the two freedoms described above, party cadres and students are now openly denied the right to believe. As one text explains:

> Ordinary citizens are permitted two freedoms. Though Party members are also citizens, they are first of all members of the party of the proletariat, and therefore *enjoy only one freedom*—the freedom not to believe—and absolutely do not enjoy the freedom to believe. They cannot have feet in two boats (XUAR Party Committee Propaganda Bureau 1997: 52, my emphasis).

This novel explication of freedom has not persuaded many people.

Students, who are theoretically also citizens, are now also limited to the single freedom in Xinjiang. Official explanations stress both the vital role of education in ensuring the future prosperity of the nation, and the importance of allowing youths of age to make a free, informed choice to believe or not to believe. For example,

> youths and children are in the growing-up stage; their world views have not yet formed. They lack scientific knowledge and life experience. They cannot yet make responsible and scientific choices appropriate to their goals. To irrigate the minds of immature youths with religious thought is to allow someone to impose belief in a particular religion on them (Luo Yingfu 1992: 171).

The author seemingly ignores the point that to prevent youths from practicing religion and others from teaching them about it is to impose unbelief. But such intervention has proven ineffectual in Xinjiang. Prosecuting religious activity and expressly forbidding the teaching of religion on school campuses in the region have not eliminated belief: a scholar noted with alarm in the mid-1990s that, when asked which was greater, the "strength of *Huda* [Allah] or the strength of science," 71 percent of high school students in Changji Prefecture sided with Allah (Gong Yong 1997: 4). Party strategists have also placed hopes on mandatory classes in atheism.

An Amnesty International report on Xinjiang claimed that the CCP began the "education in atheism" campaign in 1997.[70] Yet a textbook purchased in Kashgar demonstrates that the campaign began earlier. The text of the book makes clear that students no longer enjoy "freedom of religious belief." The fifth lesson is devoted entirely to the bald assertion that "teenagers must become atheists" (Li Ailing et al. 1992: 144 ff.).[71] Secular intellectuals, even actively antireligious ones who bemoaned the conservative influence of Islam on Uyghurs, criticized the party's intense pressure on believers.

In the mid-1990s, students at Xinjiang University were fully aware of the increasing stringency of official policy towards religious belief and observance. These students observed privately that many classmates continue to perform five prayers a day (*namaz*) and to participate secretly in study groups. But the costs of doing so were readily apparent. For instance, in spring of 1997, at the entrance to the campus computer building, a series of posters with gaudy vermillion stamps indicated that six students from Hotan had been arrested for attending religious study groups and that they had received substantial prison sentences.

Recent rumors of the spread of "Wahhabism" in southern Xinjiang have only aggravated official concern. Originating in Saudi Arabia, this strict and politically charged form of Islam has been popular among some who had previously been alienated by the party-approved version of Islam. Officials have used the term "Wahhabism" as a blanket label for all forms of radical Islamism they encounter. They worry that the spread of Islamism threatens to reverse the trend of a shrinking, and more important, increasingly politically irrelevant, religious population in Xinjiang. Investigators from the United Front Department in Hotan District claimed to have found a large number of "Wahhabist" Imams and talip there in the mid-1990s; a significant number had "bad attitudes" and a handful had committed "errors of political stance." In addition to fearing doctrinal disputes, party officials worry about religious proselytizing. Some Chinese analysts have suggested that Deng Xiaoping's reforms opened the way for problems by underscoring the freedom to join different religious sects. Reforms, they argued, "provided Wahhabism with policies favorable to its propagation." They warned that adherents have sought to wrest control of mosques from "patriotic clerics with traditional [religious] views" (Yin Zhuguang and Mao Yongfu 1996: 163, 160–61).[72] The series of assassinations of officially approved clerics in the late 1990s added to this fear.[73]

Preferential policies: affirmative action for non-Hans
Alongside the limitations of the regional autonomy system, it must be acknowledged that Xinjiang's so-called *youhui zhengce* ("preferential policies") governing family planning, education, job hiring, and cadre recruit-

ment do leave Uyghurs better off than they would otherwise have been (Sautman 1998). They can have more children, enter college with lower examination scores, find jobs in state-owned enterprises with fewer qualifications, and join some government bodies more easily than their Han counterparts in Xinjiang. These policies have unquestionably contributed to the emergence of Uyghur working and professional classes. Yet many feel that to judge the treatment of Uyghurs according to national standards is to do violence to the very premise of autonomy. Far from being "masters of their own house," they feel they have been reduced to strangers in their own land, dependent on Han governors for policy handouts and Han employers for jobs.

In truth, as a guarded defender of the policies points out, official measures fail to address the real inequalities between Hans and Uyghurs (Sautman 1998: 100–102). Though the autonomous regions were, according to Sautman, "ostensibly established to create a sense of territorial proprietorship for their autochthonous peoples," in Xinjiang Uyghurs are poorer, less urban, less likely to go to high school and college, and have fewer job prospects than Hans. Employment disparities between the two groups are particularly acute in the oil industry and in private enterprises, where officials cannot impose quotas. Uyghurs have been all but excluded from the most dynamic and profitable sectors, and thus the gap between them and Xinjiang's Han population will widen with further economic growth.

> *in Xinjiang Uyghurs are poorer, less urban, less likely to go to high school and college, and have fewer job prospects than Hans*

Economics

Economic policies enacted in Xinjiang after 1949 undeniably brought considerable benefits to the region and its inhabitants, including dramatic growth in GDP, modest industrialization, and infrastructure improvements. The economic priorities of the Mao era spread benefits widely in Xinjiang. Agricultural production increased as a consequence of land reforms and investment in irrigation, fertilizer, and mechanization. Planners set up factories for vehicle repair, machinery, cement, and textiles, as well as mines and refineries for oil and coal. State-owned enterprises provided industrial and service jobs in unprecedented numbers. Moreover, as discussed in the previous section on preferential policies, the party placed an emphasis on hiring large numbers of Uyghurs, Qazaqs, and other non-Hans. To integrate Xinjiang more tightly with China proper, the government expanded the region's network of roads, rail, and airports. Initial economic growth was enviable. GDP per capita rose from 170 yuan in 1952 to 314 yuan in 1960, though it had fallen to 229 yuan by the end of the Mao era (Weimer 2004: 169). Economic growth also brought about a general improvement in living standards, underwritten by enormous and persistent subsidies from Beijing. The subsidies did not end with the high socialist era after Mao's death in 1976 but continued into the reform era, regularly providing half of annual government expenditures and reaching nearly 12 billion yuan in 2000 (Bachman 2004: 172; Weimer 2004: 175).

But, as with the rest of the PRC, socialist economic policies had drawbacks for Xinjiang, including distorted development and the inefficient use of capital. Ill-planned and breakneck development also caused environmental degradation, including soil deterioration, desertification that often outpaced PCC land "reclamation," and a drop in the region's water table. There is some evidence that nuclear fallout from the testing at Lop Nor contaminated groundwater. Finally, in emphasizing economic integration with China proper and attempting to guard against Soviet aggression by sealing the border, the government kept Xinjiang isolated from natural markets in easy reach to the west.

Overall, the Reform era brought mixed benefits. Agricultural reforms allowed some Uyghurs (and many Hans) to prosper through specialization. Uyghurs in Turpans and nearby regions profited by cultivating melons and (especially) grapes (Rudelson 1997). Uyghur traders prospered—first from internal trade, then from transborder activities. Domestic traders traveled to China's major cities to sell fruits, raisins, walnuts, and shish kebabs. After the borders with Central Asia were reopened in the 1980s, many merchants embarked on the shuttle trade, sending textiles and housewares west and importing steel and other industrial commodities in return. Xinjiang's millionaire Uyghur businesswoman Rebiya Qadir was an early and very successful exemplar.[74] Aggregate economic growth raised per capita income considerably. By 2000, it had reached 1,699 yuan (Weimer 2004: 169).

At the same time, reform policies have exacted costs. Reforms of state-owned enterprises (SOEs) eliminated at least 600,000 jobs between 1995 and 2000 (Weimer 2004: 179). In many cases, Uyghurs appear to have been fired before Hans at SOEs (Becquelin 2000: 85). Though the state sector has continued to contribute a disproportionate share of regional GDP, private enterprise has expanded dramatically; however, Uyghurs and other non-Hans have much greater difficulty than Hans in finding jobs in the private sector. Preferential policies still officially in effect have no sway over private organizations; in fact, job advertisements and job fairs in the late 1990s indicated either explicitly or tacitly that Uyghurs "need not apply" (Gilley 2001). Interviews conducted during that period elicited many stories of Uyghur parents who paid substantial bribes to officials in hopes of securing desirable jobs for their children.[75]

The economic priorities set by government officials in the last decade appear certain to leave Uyghurs and much of southern Xinjiang further behind. The focus of production has been on "one white, one black"—in other words, on cotton and oil. Xinjiang is already the largest cotton producer in the PRC, and Beijing stipulated in 1998 that the region further expand its cotton cultivation. With state subsidies, growing cotton is profitable for large mechanized PCC farms where Hans predominate. There is evidence that cotton farming mandated by the state is leaving small-scale Uyghur cultivators worse off, as they confront high factor prices and below-market procurement prices without the protection of subsidies (Bachman 2004: 172; Becquelin 2000: 80–82). Furthermore, cotton is an extraordinarily thirsty crop. Xinjiang's water table has already dropped sixty meters over the last thirty years, and increasing cotton monoculture there will almost certainly cause further damage. The cautionary example of the Aral Sea disaster, a direct result of Khrushchev's cotton policy for Central Asia, has apparently not yet deterred Beijing planners (Toops 2004b: 272–73).[76]

As for oil, Uyghurs have long felt excluded from the industry in Xinjiang, which helps feed China's growing energy needs but whose workforce is overwhelmingly Han.[77] Many Uyghurs also feel that Xinjiang's oil and other petroleum products are their wealth and are being carted off to the interior for scandalously little compensation.[78] Xinjiang does retain a portion of the taxes on oil profits, but Uyghurs feel the region should receive at least all of the taxes and perhaps a portion of profits. It is widely believed, probably by analogy with Alaska, that exacting proper compensation for the oil would leave all wealthy.[79] Many Uyghurs are either unaware of, or choose to ignore, the huge subsidies Xinjiang has consistently received from the interior. At least one author has seen these subsidies as "a disguised form of payment" for mineral exploitation at below market rates (see also Becquelin 2000: 71–72; Pei Minxin 2002: 324). In any case, an economist has concluded on balance that, despite the subsidies and tax rebates, most of the profits from energy and mineral exploitation in Xinjiang enrich Beijing rather than the region (Weimer 2004: 174).

Most palpable in Xinjiang—but difficult to establish with accurate figures—are systematic differences in living standards between Hans and Uyghurs. There are shelves in Xinjiang's libraries and bookstores full of published statistical works comparing the Uyghur, Han, and other populations in the region on their urbanization, gender ratios, age profiles, female fertility, birth and death rates, sectoral employment, and educational attainment. But one searches in vain through all these texts for a single statistic comparing incomes among groups: it is all but impossible to find statistics on living standards broken down by *minzu*. This omission is not inadvertent, but a premeditated state policy.[80] Officials might well be seeking to avoid publicizing "negative" information that could be used to criticize the government and the system of autonomy. While state-sponsored reports do allow that "real inequalities" persist despite the establishment of "absolute legal equality," these reports studiously avoid putting numbers to those gaps.

However, one can approximate group per capita incomes by correlating statistics on living standards categorized by region with the population distributions in those regions. Several analysts of Xinjiang have remarked on the strong coincidence of high incomes with high concentrations of Hans as well as low incomes with Uyghur predominance (Bachman 2004: 165–68; Toops 2004a: 261–62). Using regression analysis to tease out systematic differences in incomes, an economist has found that each 1 percent increase in Han population in a district adds an increment of 44 yuan to per capita income (Weimer 2004: 177).

In sum, there is hard evidence that Uyghurs have fallen behind Hans economically in the Reform era, and every reason to believe the gap will widen.[81] This gap can be attributed in part to structural or systemic causes. Hiring patterns in key state and private industries have been at best discriminatory and often exclusionary; one analyst has suggested that the economy shifted from "discriminat[ory]" to "segregative" over the 1990s (Becquelin 2000: 90). Another analyst argues that the developmental policies applied to Xinjiang "can only be seen as Han economic imperialism" (Bachman 2004: 156).

Choices by many Uyghurs have probably also contributed to enduring inequalities. It is widely known that Uyghurs are as a group less educated than Hans, but few have attempted to account for this difference (Hannum and Xie 1998). Uyghur families, particularly those in predominantly agrarian southern Xinjiang, may place less emphasis on education than their Han counterparts, though educational fees and linguistic pressures may also drive some pupils away. In addition, some Uyghurs are by their own account not interested in jobs with long hours and rigid work discipline.[82]

Pressures for change

As noted above, Uyghur dissatisfaction with the political system in Xinjiang has been manifest since the founding of the PRC. Pressures to change the legal framework or the policies on autonomy have also come from other sources: Soviet bloc writers and officials, softline Xinjiang officials urging the expansion of autonomy, and hardliners demanding its reduction. In the last decade, industrialized democracies and international organizations have also begun to scrutinize the system and press for change through moral suasion.

Marxists inside and outside China condemned the framework of autonomy from very early on. Following the Sino-Soviet split, Soviet authors scornfully denounced China's system of autonomous regions as a betrayal of socialist principles. One argued that Beijing had denied non-Hans their "legal right to self-determination," while another complained that the government had offered them "only a truncated territorial autonomy" (Connor 1984: 236).

Deng Xiaoping was aware that this was still a live issue in the 1980s, as a comment he made that only recently came to light reveals: "Xinjiang's fundamental question is [whether it should be] a republic or an autonomous region." Echoing Zhou Enlai's 1957 remarks, Deng asserted that "we're different from the Soviet Union, we can't have a republic; we are [sic] an autonomous region."[83] As had Zhou, Deng defended the Chinese system against Soviet-bloc criticisms, boasting in 1987 to Hungary's Janos Kadar that, while the Chinese government had chosen not to have a Soviet-style federation of republics, the country's system of autonomous regions was one of the best points of China's socialist system and must not be abandoned (Zhu Peimin 2000: 334, 337).

Party theorists wrote lengthy treatises to lay to rest the criticism of its system of autonomy. For instance, in a work billed as the first account of China's system of regional autonomy that integrated Marxist-Leninist theory and Chinese practice, the author acknowledged the CCP's gradual abandonment of the principle of self-determination, but claimed it was entirely justified. The CCP did indeed "emphasize many times and over a long period the principle of the right to *minzu* self-determination," though it ceased to do so after the victory over the Japanese in 1945. The CCP's support of the principle of self-determination in the 1930s and 1940s was "understandable" given its membership in the Communist Third International; so was its "use of the slogan of *minzu* self-determination" to motivate non-Hans to fight against imperialism. But the author also defended the government's decision in September 1949—as the Chinese People's Political Consultative Conference deliberated on the shape of New China—to entirely abandon the principle of self-determination for *minzu.* The repudiation of self-determination at that point, he wrote, was "correct" and "a matter of course" because it would simply have served imperialist plans to split up China (Zhang Erju 1988: 33–36).[84] Official scholars adopted a still firmer line in 1999, declaring that "to pursue 'self-determination' [in contemporary Xinjiang] is to engage in splittism" (Pan Zhiping 1999: 178–81).

These official comments and theoretical works have clearly been intended to answer Marxist critiques of the politico-legal framework of autonomy. While neither silenced those critiques, Chinese officials can observe with bittersweet satisfaction that many of the critics have lost their jobs, and in several cases their countries. CCP officials often point to the disintegration of the Soviet Union and Yugoslavia as proof that Mao and his cohort made prudent choices in 1949. More recently, Beijing has faced criticisms from various foreign governments and NGOs about the actual workings of the system and the true degree of autonomy in Xinjiang. Meanwhile, Uyghurs have continued to clamor for more substantial self-rule.[85]

Uyghurs have continued to clamor for more substantial self-rule

A few officials and scholars at the beginning of the Reform era had already been acknowledging the limitations and even the failures of the system of autonomy's implementation. These doubts were revealed, for example, in the recently published report of a group of specialists on *minzu* problems (a group that would have included a large number of non-Hans) who were trading ideas at a symposium on that topic in Beijing in 1980. Despite the party's proclivity for "emphasizing the positive," an occasional critical note slipped through at the symposium. It was the consensus of the conferees that

> [t]he principal problem at present is that the powers of self-government and decision making powers pertaining to the policy of *minzu* regional autonomy have not yet really been implemented (*wei neng zhizheng de luoshi*)...
>
> Some comrades noted that *minzu* equality has not yet been successfully established in people's minds, compromising the implementation of decisionmaking authority. There are those who see *minzu* regions purely as "materials supply sites," and seldom concern themselves with the economic development of [those regions]; they infringe upon the legitimate interests of *minzu* regions. The problem of nativization of organs of self-government has for quite a few years now, and especially during the time of the "gang of four," become a virtual taboo. The proportion of *minzu* cadres in self-government organs has fallen drastically, producing a situation in which "minority *minzu* manage household affairs (*dangjia*), Hans make the decisions (*zuozhu*)" (Anonymous 1981: 78).

But public acknowledgment of the problem did not bring about much change, as we have seen. In 1988, the author of an officially supported national study admitted with concern that most non-Han groups continued to be underrepresented in governments of the autonomous regions, as reflected in the disparity between cadre ratios and population ratios. He argued that this was a critical problem for the system's implementation. Without a substantial body of non-Han cadres, he wrote, "the true realization of...autonomy is impossible." His suggested solution was to train non-Han cadres in large numbers (Zhang Erju 1988: 287). As discussed above, this suggestion has not had much effect.

A dominant group of high officials appears to have viewed renewed calls for nativization with suspicion. As noted, many officials believed that the looser and more tolerant policies enacted under Hu Yaobang *caused* the demonstrations and violence of the 1980s and 1990s. Furthermore, many argued that the criticism of the Cultural Revolution's leftist extremes had provided cover for the emergence of ethnonationalist extremism. Policy advisor Ma Dazheng cited as evidence a letter submitted to the Xinjiang government in 1980.[86] The letter's author complained that "in Xinjiang, the leadership of the party has always meant leadership by Han cadres." To remedy the situation, the author proposed setting ratios for cadres. "Xinjiang is the Uyghur autonomous region," the author wrote. "This point absolutely must not be forgotten or overlooked. Therefore...Uyghur cadres should constitute no less than 45 percent of the total (not less than 60 percent in southern Xinjiang) and cadres from the AR's other minority *minzu* should make up not less than 15 percent."

Reading the letter almost two decades later in 1998, Ma was disturbed by two aspects of its argument. First, its call for "full autonomy" smacked of "*minzu* attitude." This concerned him particularly because Kosovar Albanians had recently raised the standard of full autonomy to cloak their ultimate aim of full independence. Second, in the two decades since the letter had been written, Ma said, its spirit had developed into an "erroneous intellectual current" and had spread among the masses (understood to be Uyghur), making them susceptible to incitement and organization by separatists (Ma Dazheng 2003: 185–86).

Facing pressures for more autonomy in Xinjiang, hardliners have instead recently pushed measures to diminish its scope. These measures include stimulating increased Han immigration and *reducing* the proportion of non-Han cadres by recruiting more Hans to the region: "Hanization" instead of nativization. Policy advisors on *minzu* affairs to the Xinjiang government argued in the mid-1990s that Han flight and more relaxed family planning controls on non-Hans had done damage to the balance of populations in the region. They urged the government to adopt "special policies" to remedy the "out-of-balance population ratio [by] inducing some Han cadres and members of the masses to volunteer to come to Xinjiang...." These advisors nevertheless worried that policies could not swiftly bring about radical change in the region's population ratios (Mao Yongfu and Li Ling 1996: 180). It requires little wit to infer that officials have long had target ratios in mind.

In a work intended for internal circulation among policy elites, Ma Dazheng made a more searching critique of the Uyghur agitation for more representative government and politics. It was not just the ratios themselves that were troubling, wrote Ma, but non-Hans' focus on them. Directly contradicting policy analysts of the decade earlier, he argued against equating cadre ratios with autonomy. To do so, in fact, carried a grave risk: "[T]he minute one raises 'autonomy' in Xinjiang, people, and especially comrades from minority *minzu,* think immediately of the question of ratios of cadres and civil servants. The two have practically become synonyms. This has become a 'big and intractable problem' difficult for local governments to resolve." In fact, he continued, the question of ratios had become fertile "soil for 'ethnocentrism.'" Ma repeatedly proposed recruiting still more Han cadres, though he urged that local Hans be chosen in preference over those from China proper. He also urged the government to make a test of political loyalty the condition of continued government service for cadres, and to dismiss those who fail (Ma Dazheng 2003: 124, 188–89). The government's retreat from the language of definite ratios is subtle but plain. By the late 1990s, in calling for the training of "politically aware minority *minzu* cadres able to correctly implement Party policies," Jiang Zemin announced simply that China must have *yi pi* ("a group") of them (Huang Guangxue 2001).

Some scholars have even obliquely suggested abandoning the commitment to autonomy altogether, although they certainly did so with official support. In the reform era, academics and low-level functionaries have often published theoretical essays that float ideas being contemplated within the government. This provides what Americans now refer to wryly as "plausible deniability" for potentially unpopular actions. Thus the young scholar Zhu Lun, researcher in the *Minzu* Institute of the Chinese Academy of Social Sciences, asserted in 2002 that the idea of autonomy was obsolete and no longer suited to global realities. Collective rule (*gongzhi*)[87] is now the "basic tenet of *minzu* politics in contemporary multi-*minzu* states," he argued. Zhu proposed that policymakers instead begin to think about *hou zizhi* ("post-autonomy") (Zhu Lun 2002: 4, 6).

In China, if a scholarly article is followed by a similar one soon thereafter, it strengthens the supposition that the original article's idea had official support. Indeed, commenting several months later on Zhu's article, legal scholar Du Wenzhong argued that "China's praxis for resolving problems of *minzu* relations should be understood as a praxis of *gongzhi* ['collective rule']." Chinese jurisprudential scholars' continued use of the term *zizhi* ("autonomy") to describe *minzu* policies was not only unwise but "inaccurate." In reality, Du maintained, the newly amended Law on Regional Autonomy stipulated "collective rule" by the state and local autonomous organs (Du Wenzhong 2002: 8). This idea was echoed in policy proposals made specifically for Xinjiang, once again by Ma Dazheng. Prior work on the theory of *minzu* policies, the author argued, had "put too great an emphasis on *minzu* autonomy...," which ought to be balanced by a greater emphasis on "collective rule" (Ma Dazheng 2003: 188–89).

Conclusion

To suggest that Chinese policies in Xinjiang have been a key source of conflict is to imply that things might have been different. Historical counterfactuals are a notoriously shaky ground for comparison. Furthermore, the frequency of ethnic conflict and violence in Xinjiang during the Republican era might have led us to expect both to continue after 1949. The argument here is not that a suite of ideal policies would have eliminated discontent and friction entirely. But had the CCP hewed more closely to what Hannum and Lillich (1980) described as the minimal principles of autonomy, there would have been less conflict in the region; and the particular departures of Chinese practice from that minimal model exacerbated conflict in particular ways.

These problems did not originate at the regional level. As Pei Minxin argued recently, two features of China's national political system have "in reality allowed almost no genuine local autonomy." First, Beijing has kept power strongly centralized; second, party leaders have adamantly opposed substantial democratization, which might have allowed the articulation of and bargaining over local demands. These tendencies remain obstacles to beneficial changes. At the same time, Pei suggested that China's system of *minzu* regional autonomy has been in crisis since the mid-1990s. The country's market transition has dramatically reduced Beijing's capacity to redistribute resources and therefore to subsidize the less developed border regions. In addition, wrote Pei, international scrutiny has placed greater restraints on Beijing's use of repression or state-sponsored migration. Finally, in recent years, repression has proven less effective and more explosive in regions like Xinjiang and Tibet (Pei Minxin 2002: 319–21, 323, 327).

While these points are well taken, this paper has argued that the crisis in Xinjiang began brewing decades ago. As we now know, the backlash against repression in the region had already begun in the 1950s, and the refusal by leaders in Beijing and Ürümci to allow open expression of dissatisfaction has only increased it. Repeated and harsh clampdowns on demonstrations have left the field of overt political action to the violent and desperate. Massive and multifaceted repression of religion has made its practice far more political than it need have been. The pattern of regional economic development has also ensured the further segmentation of the labor market, a segmentation that is often blamed elsewhere in the world for strengthening oppositional identities and aggravating intergroup friction.[88] The mining and export of Xinjiang's oil and gas by an almost entirely Han workforce and according to Beijing's dictates instead of through explicit bargaining all increase Uyghurs' sense that their region's resources are being expropriated. Heavy Han immigration and the continuous choice of Han officials for the most powerful government and party positions strengthens Uyghurs' perception of invasion and alien rule. Finally, Han immigration and state policies have dramatically increased the pressure on Uyghurs to assimilate linguistically and culturally, seemingly contradicting the explicit protections of the constitution and the laws on autonomy and making the cultural divide yet more pronounced.

Hardline Chinese officials have frequently argued that only these harsh policies have averted Xinjiang's secession. Once again, it is difficult to argue the historical counterfactual. And as with other groups of comparable size, the more than 8.5 million Uyghurs surely differ amongst themselves. They are divided by urban and rural distinctions, differences of wealth, regional loyalties, and attitudes about the proper role of Islam in public life. Without representative and unbiased information about the aspirations of Uyghurs from all corners of Xinjiang, from every class and social group, it is all but impossible to know whether increased autonomy would satisfy the majority.[89] But less severe policies would certainly have provoked less desperation and violence.

Chinese officials could have granted broader cultural and religious latitude in Xinjiang. They need not have punished Uyghur dissidents so severely over the last half century. Policymakers could have done more to ensure Uyghurs were more fully incorporated into the economy, and on a broadly equal footing with Hans. Beijing could certainly have granted Uyghurs and other non-Hans much more authority in government and party. And the state need not have forced the immigration of so many Hans to the region during the Mao era.

These policies can still be ameliorated now—even with respect to the complex matter of immigration. Though many Uyghurs would clearly like to place limits on voluntary Han immigration today, to do so would compromise both Chinese sovereignty and individual Chinese citizens' right to freedom of movement. Critics are on much firmer ground in opposing "preferential packages" for immigrant Han farmers, plans to subsidize the expansion of the PCC, and the intentional importation of Han bureaucrats from the interior to rule China's Uyghur regions. Sadly, the September 11 attacks and their aftermath have clearly relaxed the international constraints on the repressive policies of Beijing identified by Pei Minxin, who wrote slightly before that pivotal event. The announcement of the global "war on terror" has probably emboldened Beijing to respond to dissent by tightening its grip on the region, and thus to diminish further the small amount of autonomy Uyghurs and others currently exercise. The apparent plan to reduce the scope of autonomy is avoidable and certain to further exacerbate discontent.

Endnotes

1. Portions of this article appeared in a chapter published in Morris Rossabi, ed., <u>Governing China's Multiethnic Frontiers</u>, (Seattle: University of Washington Press, 2004). For advice on this version, the author would like to thank Muthiah Alagappa, Chu Shulong, Harold Crouch, Arienne Dwyer, Arun Swamy, Nury Turkel, and various members of the East-West Center project on Internal Conflicts in Asia. Special thanks to Muthiah Alagappa and the three anonymous reviewers for extraordinarily valuable criticism and suggestions. The article draws on 22 months of field work conducted between 1994 and 2002. The author gratefully acknowledges research support from the National Science Foundation, the Cornell Peace Studies Program, the MacArthur Foundation, and the Washington University Political Science Department. Note that phrases in Mandarin Chinese are written in italics, while those in Uyghur are underlined.

2. This article gives comparatively little attention to political sentiments of the more than one million Qazaqs and the several million members of several other non-Han groups who call Xinjiang home. On Xinjiang's Qazaqs, see Benson and Svanberg (1988); Benson and Svanberg (1998).

3. Moseley (1965: 16). Cited in Shakya (1999: 306).

4. I join with a number of scholars in preferring to leave the Chinese word "*minzu*" untranslated. Dictionaries offer as translations, variously, "ethnic group," "nationality," and "nation". Since these English terms carry such different political connotations, and since in Chinese the term is functionally ambiguous, I intentionally leave the term in Chinese throughout.

5. For discussions of the impact of state policies on Uyghur identity, see Gladney (1990), Rudelson (1997), and Bovingdon (1998; 2002b). Scholars have similarly implicated the state in the formation of collective identities among Hui (Gladney 1991) and Zhuang (Kaup 2000).

6. For concise treatments of politics in Mongolia, Ningxia, and Tibet, see the various chapters in Rossabi (2004); on Guangxi, see Kaup (2000).

7. One must add that misrule by Chinese overlords permitted (or perhaps set the tone for) similar misrule by local Uyghur officials (Forbes 1986).

8. See accounts of politics under autocratic states in general (Scott 1985; Scott 1990), in the USSR and Eastern Europe (Kuran 1992; Laitin 1991), and in Xinjiang (Bovingdon 2002b).

9. For a journalistic account of anger about nuclear testing and oil exploitation in the mid-1990s, see Chen (1994a).

10. Most information in the paragraph is from Shichor (2004: 138–40); the Chinese source is Wang (1999: 195). There is also considerable evidence that the Soviet invasion of Afghanistan led the Chinese to train anti-Soviet mujahedin in Xinjiang in the 1980s. Some have seen both the rise of violence in Xinjiang in the 1990s and the discovery of a small number of Uyghurs fighting among the Taliban in Afghanistan 2002 as unintended consequences of this training.

11. For a fuller account of transnational Uyghur organizations, see Shichor (2001); Gladney (2004); and Millward (2004).

12. Fieldnotes, 2002.

13. See, for example, Xu Yuqi (1999: 2–3), Wang Shuanqian (1999: 198).

14. Colin Mackerras suggests Zhou's speech was not published at the time because it ran afoul of the "prevailing ideological trend," but that by 1980 it was quite consonant with Deng Xiaoping's policy aims (Mackerras 1994: 154).

15. Former XUAR governor Säypidin recalls that, in 1955, leaders in Beijing had initially proposed calling the region simply the "Xinjiang Autonomous Region." Säypidin objected that "[a]utonomy is not given to mountains and rivers. It is given to particular nationalities. I do not think the name...is really appropriate." He was gratified to learn, several days later, that Mao had agreed with him, insisting it be the "Xinjiang Uyghur Autonomous Region" (Foreign Broadcast Information Service-China Daily Report (hereafter referred to as FBIS-CHI) 95–221, November 16, 1995: 89–90). He does not record his reaction to the 1951 "Uyghurstan" controversy discussed above (Zhu Peimin 2000: 335).

16. In 1955, according to official statistics, the 3.72 million Uyghurs comprised roughly 73 percent of the region's total population of 5.11 million.

17. The data in this paragraph come from Yin Zhuguang and Mao Yongfu (1996: 132–33).

18. I am grateful to Chris Atwood for the reference. To be sure, Mongols had faced similarly flagrant gerrymandering in their "home districts" long before 1949, and would see the shape of their "autonomous region" manipulated several times in the PRC period. They were vastly outnumbered by Hans from the founding of the Inner Mongolia Autonomous Region in 1947—see Bulag (2004: 90–92). For a particularly lucid discussion of territorial manipulations in ethnographic Tibet, see Shakya (1999).

19. Mao Yongfu was director of the Policy Research Office, XUAR CCP committee. See David Wang (1998: 52 n. 60).

20. For an explanation of the rationale for establishing nested autonomies, and a description of the process through which the Xinjiang Autonomous Region was established, see Säypidin's recollection in 1995, published in *People's Daily* 28 September 1995, translation in FBIS-CHI-95–221, November 16, 1995: 85–91. A recent online article argues that "using Hui, Mongols, and Qazaqs to rule Uyghurs" was precisely what motivated officials to divide the territory thus. See (XueYu (pseudonym: Snowy Regions) 2003).

21. Residents of Xinjiang refer to all Chinese provinces to the east as *neidi* ("the interior"). To avoid confusion, I render this idea with the once-popular term "China proper" (*Zhongguo ben bu* in Chinese).

22. Unmentioned (because beyond question) was obedience to Party organs at equivalent and higher levels.

23. Here *renmin* ("the people") was understood to denote only a portion of the total population. The party-state retained the right to determine which people belonged to "the people" and who were class enemies or enemies of the state. For the text of the Program, see Li Weihan (1982: 521–26).

24. References in this paragraph are to the amended 2001 law, though the relevant articles are almost indistinguishable from those in the 1984 law. The most substantial change of interest here is in Article 20, which has added a requirement that the higher-level government organ respond to proposed alterations within 60 days. According to an article in an official journal, the amendment committee made this change because the provision for local modification of national policies had "essentially not been enacted." Superior governments that were presented such proposals by autonomous governments routinely "set them aside and ignored them, never providing a response" (Ao Junde 2001).

25. Though the constitution and Autonomy Law explicitly allow autonomous regions to pass such statutes, Xinjiang's government has never done so (Ghalip Isma'il 1996).

26. Yu received his BA in China and his LLM and SJD from Harvard; he has published extensively on Chinese constitutional matters. He has been a visiting professor at Beijing University and now teaches at Chinese University of Hong Kong. This working paper is available at his CUHK webpage, cited in the bibliography.

27. Moneyhon makes these points with specific reference to Xinjiang. The Autonomy Law he analyzes applies to all autonomous regions in China from the provincial level down, and Beijing has chosen all the executives of the five autonomous regions since 1949.

28. For a concise introduction to the political and demographic legacies of an even earlier period, see Millward (2000). For English-language works that cover the modern political history of Xinjiang, see Fletcher (1978), Forbes (1986), Benson (1990), and David Wang (1999). Millward and Tursun (2004) offer a reliable and remarkably concise version of that history.

29. I refer to the paramilitary farms interchangeably as *bingtuan* and the Production and Construction Corps (PCC). On the PCC, see Dreyer (1994); Esposito (1974); McMillen (1981); McMillen (1984); McMillen (1979); and Seymour (2000).

30. Tibet, Inner Mongolia, and other non-Han regions also had "Anti-local nationalist campaigns."

31. A Qazaq who had fled Xinjiang in 1962 claimed in 1963 to head a Soviet-sponsored guerrilla army of 60,000, staffed by refugees from the region and preparing to attack China (Mackerras 1994: 172).

32. Interview, Ürümci, October 23, 1996. See also Rudelson (1997: 104). Dru Gladney learned of forced pig-raising in Hui regions as well, and attributes it to socialist enthusiasm; harder to explain are episodes in which Hui were forced to eat pork, or watched in dismay as pork bones were thrown into their wells (Gladney 1991: 135, 138).

33. William C. Clark, "Ibrahim's Story" (unpublished manuscript): 17.

34. Interviews, Ürümci, October 10, 1996 and April 1, 1997.

35. Hu made these suggestions before traveling to Xinjiang. He later visited the region twice en route to Europe, once in 1983 and again in 1986, and made a formal two-week inspection tour in summer 1985 (Zhu Peimin 2000: 359–60).

36. This passage quotes from and paraphrases Dillon (2004: 36). Dillon in turn cites the official's quotation from Ruan Ming, "Missed Historic Opportunity Recalled," *Minzhu Zhongguo* 8 (February 1992), 17–18, Paris, Translated in JPRS-CAR-92-039.

37. For another account of Beijing's combined "hard and soft policies" in Xinjiang, see Rudelson and Jankowiak (2004: 301–2).

38. Though Beijing had initiated the "Strike Hard" campaign in 1983 to combat the rising national crime rate and repeated sweeps periodically in the intervening years, a special Xinjiang-specific Strike Hard campaign was announced in April 1996 (Dillon 2004: 84-5; Tanner 1999). Amnesty International (1999) and other human rights organizations claim that officials have used Strike Hard to arrest suspected separatists, convict them in kangaroo courts, and imprison or execute them at lightning speed.

39. A dictionary of "new Chinese terms" explains *zonghe zhili* as steps taken "to resolve problems of social order...using political, economic, ideological, educational, cultural, administrative, legal, and other measures, to attack evil trends, crimes, illegality, and breaches of discipline…" (Wen Hui, Wang Peng, and Li Bengang 1992: 676). The term has since been replaced with *zonghe zhengzhi* ("comprehensive political rectification").

40. Fieldnotes, 1997. Anti-separatist propaganda sweeps have continued. See "China reports popular support for propaganda work in Xinjiang's Ili region" (2000), and a similar report by BBC News Online (May 29, 2000), available online at http://news.bbc.co.uk/hi/english/world/asia-pacific/newsid_768000/768815.stm, accessed on April 11, 2001.

41. See Agence France Press (2000). On the 2001 addition of Uzbekistan to the organization, henceforth called the "Shanghai Cooperation Organization," see Xinhua (2001).

42. A document promulgated by China's State Council on January 21, 2002 made the case with detailed descriptions of violence over the previous decade (Guowuyuan xinwen bangongshi 2002), though as Millward (2004) has argued few of the examples fit the category of terrorism.

43. Fieldnotes, summer 2002; Lim (2003); see also Gladney (2004).

44. Melvyn Goldstein argued not long ago that Beijing has chosen similar strategies for Tibet, and for similar reasons. Its plans for economic development and Han immigration are intended to alter Tibet so dramatically that "failure to win over a new generation of Tibetans will not weaken Beijing's control over Tibet" (Goldstein 1997: 110). Tsering Shakya suggests that Tibetan officials tacitly agreed to Han immigration despite widespread opposition from ordinary Tibetans (Shakya 1999: 438).

45. A poignant news broadcast from March 1981 chronicled the flight of several individuals back to Shanghai and their subsequent return to Xinjiang under heavy government pressure. In each case, party officials in Shanghai patiently explained the harm they caused Xinjiang and the importance of their returning to continue the work of "reclaiming the wastelands." FBIS-CHI-81-061, March 31, 1981: T4.

46. The system registered each citizen as a resident of a particular locale, and gave urban residents access to ration coupons only in that region. The system made it nearly impossible for peasants to move to cities. Urban residents could not change their registration to a new locale without an invitation from a work unit there and a release from the home unit, both extremely hard to obtain. Without changed registration, people could not obtain ration coupons and therefore faced great difficulty purchasing food and other necessities.

47. China News Digest, April 2, 2001, consulted online at www.cnd.org.

48. "GMRB interviews Xinjiang Party Secretary on Talented People in Western Region," FBIS #20040102000054. I am grateful to Warren Smith for this reference.

49. A recent state-sponsored study justifies the implementation of birth restrictions among non-Hans with economic logic: "The excessive speed with which Xinjiang's population is growing directly affects the increase in per capita incomes." The book also defends birth restrictions on the basis of eugenic and ecological principles, and takes care to point out that the non-Han population is growing more rapidly than that of Hans. It does not mention that immigration has contributed directly to both the rate of growth and the absolute size of the population, or that the Han population in Xinjiang grew at many times the rate of the non-Han population for several decades. (Xu Xifa 1995: 23–24, 170).

50. Fieldnotes, 1994, 1995, 2002.

51. There were PCC regiments originally in Mongolia and other "border" regions (e.g., Bulag 2000: 182–83; He Gang and Shi Weimin 1994). All but those in Xinjiang were subsequently disbanded.

52. The overall population figure is from Xinjiang Weiwuer Zizhiqu Tongjiju (1995: 46). 1974 figures are from Zhang Erju et al. (1988: 241); 1994 figures are from XUAR local gazetteer editorial committee (1995: 499). It is highly likely that a substantial proportion of the remaining 11.7 percent were not native to Xinjiang; official statisticians routinely fold all 55 non-Han groups into the category "*minzu*" in such charts.

53. No less an authority than Deng Xiaoping acknowledged that "The Xinjiang Production and Construction Corps...serves as an important force in maintaining local stability..." (quoted in Seymour 2000: 182). Seymour remarks that "the central government...seemed to have more confidence in it as a bulwark against minority nationalism than it had in the XUAR government..." (181).

54. Uradyn Bulag (2004: 100) makes a similar argument about Mongol officials in Inner Mongolia. In the Soviet Union, Gregory Gleason observes, Moscow selected "pliant local leaders" to provide an "aura of local representation" in the union republics while staving off the emergence of nationalism (1990: 88).

55. Note that my switching back and forth between "Uyghur" and "non-Han" is intentional. Official figures typically identify all *minzu* (meaning all "minority *minzu*) cadres as a bloc, to blur the distinctions among groups and to inflate the figures adduced to prove a high degree of indigenous control. A fully assimilated Bai or Manchu serving in Ürümci or Ghulja counts as a *minzu* cadre.

56. "Th[e] figures indicated a definite Han predominance on the upper and middle-level Party committees in the region" (McMillen 1979: 75–76). Guo Zhengli (1992: 89) also acknowledges that the real situation of non-Han cadre recruitment is "quite uneven; [among] its principal manifestations is the scarcity of non-Han core cadres (*gugan ganbu*) at the county level and above...."

57. Not all cadres hold positions of political authority. One scholar-official notes with concern that nearly 40 percent of non-Han cadres in the late 1990s were elementary and middle school teachers (Yang Faren 2000: 160)

58. Figures are calculated from *Xinjiang Nianjian* (Xinjiang Yearbook), editions from 1988 and 1995. As with non-Russian groups in the Soviet Union that were underrepresented in the party, there are three plausible explanations: either the party considered them politically suspect, or they were averse to joining, or both. See Armstrong (1992: 243).

59. Interview, May 1997.

60. Fieldnotes, 1996, 1997.

61. Interview, December 1996.

62. "Scar literature" depicted the violence and personal suffering inflicted by the Cultural Revolution. Democratic activists pasted broadsides on "Democracy Wall" in Beijing in 1978 and 1979, until Deng Xiaoping shut down the movement and imprisoned some prominent dissidents, including Wei Jingsheng.

63. Interviews conducted in the summer of 2002 revealed *Motherland* had done precisely that.

64. Fieldnotes, summer 2002; Dillon (2002). For more on banned publications, see Bovingdon and Tursun (2004).

65. I came to this conclusion on the basis of months spent with Uyghurs watching television, listening to songs and poems, and reacting to passages of books, magazines, or newspapers. In gatherings, Uyghurs would often compete to heap scorn on official speeches or celebrate episodes in which other Uyghurs had "talked back to power." For more evidence, see Smith (2000: 209-10); Bovingdon (2002a).

66. On the Dai, see Hansen (1999); on the Hui, Gladney (1991); Lipman (1997). Matthew Kapstein describes in the case of Tibet "twin phenomena of increasing freedom and continuing repression..." (Kapstein 2004: 261).

67. By one estimate, there had been over 12,000 mosques in Kashgar Prefecture and 126 in Kashgar City in the early 1950s (Dillon 2004: 28).

68. It is striking that avowedly atheist officials could claim to understand the needs of religious citizens—particularly given that, since 1949, the population of the "believing masses" in Kashgar had nearly doubled, while a decade of reconstruction had only restored three-quarters the original number of mosques.

69. An Arabic term meaning "religious pupil," now well known in its plural form *taliban*.

70. See Amnesty International (1999), fn. 52.

71. The book's publishing information indicates it came out in 1992, in a print run of at least 79,000 volumes. The introduction indicates that the book was written in Chinese in 1991 in response to calls from the 3rd XUAR Party Congress, 15th plenum, to deal with the threat of "*minzu* splittism," and translated into Uyghur within six months. It was prepared for use in political study classes at the high-school level.

72. The term "*biaoxian*," familiar to students of Chinese politics, is difficult to render into English. Technically, it refers not to attitude but to "expression" of attitude. Those with good *biaoxian* are regarded as more reliable by party functionaries, and individuals with particularly good *biaoxian* are rewarded with promotions and other perks. See Walder (1986).

73. The Chinese State Council provided a list of assassinations in its "January 21" document (Guowuyuan xinwen bangongshi 2002).

74. On her trading success, see Chen (1994b). Rebiya Qudir was the same person imprisoned in 2000 on the charge of sending "state secrets" to her husband in the United States. Her patronym is often miswritten as "Kadeer" because that is how the Chinese government transliterates her name in Mandarin.

75. Fieldnotes 1996, 1997.

76. The figure on the region's declining water table is from Hagt (2003).

77. In 1994, an official openly admitted the industry hired few Uyghurs, claiming "most can't meet the basic standards" (Chen 1994a).

78. It is important to note that every PRC constitution has stipulated that subsurface minerals are the property of China's whole population, not that of a region or group.

79. Fieldnotes 1994, 1995, 1996, 2002.

80. Nor can this choice be attributed to party concern about a particularly volatile region. Such statistics are closely guarded even in the most peaceful and least politicized of the autonomous regions, the Guangxi Zhuang Autonomous Region. Researcher Katherine Kaup learned in interviews that officials were forbidden to publish figures comparing Han and Zhuang incomes (Kaup 2000: 150 and n. 2).

81. Hannum and Yu (1998) came to the same conclusion by studying the data from the 1982 and 1990 PRC censuses. They found that, compared with Hans, Uyghurs were overrepresented in agriculture and underrepresented in industry and service sectors, and that these imbalances had grown more pronounced over the interval. Given the increasing importance of education to financial success and continuing differences in educational levels across the same period, they projected that such inequalities would persist.

82. Fieldnotes 1997, 2002.

83. Deng's remarks from a 1981 conversation with Xinjiang's Second Party Secretary Gu Jingsheng were published in the *Xinjiang Daily* newspaper in 1998. Officials probably decided to publish the remarks 17 years later as part of the plan to win public support for the struggle against separatists.

84. For a theoretical work justifying CCP choices with specific reference to Xinjiang, see Guo Zhengli (1992).

85. See Becquelin (2000); Bovingdon (2002b); Gladney (2002); Gladney (2004); Rudelson (1997); and Smith (2000).

86. Ma Dazheng straddles the worlds of scholar and official. Widely published on historical topics, he has for nearly 15 years headed the Center for Borderlands Geographical and Historical Research (*bianjiang shi di yanjiusuo*) at the Chinese Academy of Social Sciences. The institute houses scholars researching a wide variety of historical topics. Ma and other members also spend considerable time traveling the country, advising civilian and military officials on threats to China's borders. The policy work cited below is the internally published record of research assigned to Ma by leaders at the highest level.

87. In an author's note, Zhu proposed the unfortunate English neologism "jointnomy" to render *gongzhi.*

88. The classic articulation of the argument is found in Hechter (1975). Though not without its critics, Hechter's theory of "internal colonialism" has spawned a rich secondary literature, including a debate over whether Xinjiang is an internal colony. See Gladney (1998); Sautman (2000).

89. The early survey work of Ji Ping (1990) and Herbert Yee's ambitious recent research (2003) certainly make a start toward a full picture of Uyghur sentiment. Nevertheless, since both studies were conducted with the approval and (we must assume) under the supervision of the state, they cannot be considered fully representative or unbiased. Timur Kuran (1992) has argued that any information collected about popular attitudes under repressive, autocratic regimes is bound to be distorted.

Bibliography

Agence France Press. 2000. "Russia, China, Central Asian states to boost military ties." March 30.

Amnesty International. 1999. *Gross Violations of Human Rights in the Xinjiang Uighur Autonomous Region.* London: Amnesty International.

Ao Junde. 2001. "Minzu quyu zizhifa shi zenyang xiugai de" (How the law on minzu regional autonomy was amended). *Zhongguo minzu (China Ethnicity)* (4).

Armstrong, John A. 1992. "The Ethnic Scene in the Soviet Union: The View of the Dictatorship." *In The Soviet Nationality Reader: The Disintegration in Context,* ed. R. Denber. Boulder: Westview.

Atwood, Christopher P. 2004. *Encyclopedia of Mongolia and the Mongol Empire.* New York: Facts on File.

BBC. 2000. "China reports popular support for propaganda work in Xinjiang's Ili region." *BBC Monitoring Asia Pacific-Political,* February 17.

Bachman, David. 2004. "Making Xinjiang Safe for the Han? Contradictions and Ironies of Chinese Governance in China's Northwest." *In Governing China's Multiethnic Frontiers,* ed. M. Rossabi. Seattle: University of Washington Press.

Becquelin, Nicolas. 2000. "Xinjiang in the Nineties." *The China Journal* 44: 65–90.

Benson, Linda. 1990. *The Ili Rebellion: the Moslem Challenge to Chinese Authority in Xinjiang, 1944–49.* Armonk: M.E. Sharpe.

Benson, Linda, and Ingvar Svanberg. 1988. "The Kazaks in Xinjiang." In *The Kazaks of China: Essays on an Ethnic Minority,* ed. L. Benson and I. Svanberg. Uppsala: Almquist and Wiksell International.

Benson, Linda, and Ingvar Svanberg, eds. 1998. *China's Last Nomads: The History and Culture of China's Kazaks.* Armonk: M. E. Sharpe.

Bovingdon, Gardner. 1998. "From *Qumulluq* to *Uyghur*: The Role of Education in the Development of a Pan-Uyghur Identity." *Journal of Central Asian Studies* 3(1): 19–29.

———. 2001. "The History of the History of Xinjiang." *Twentieth Century China* 26(2): 95–139.

———. 2002a. "The Not-so-silent Majority: Uyghur Resistance to Han Rule in Xinjiang." *Modern China* 28(1): 39–78.

———. 2002b. Strangers in Their Own Land: The Politics of Uyghur Identity in Chinese Central Asia. Ph. D. dissertation, Government, Cornell University, Ithaca.

———. n.d. *Bodies in Excess: The State and Islam in China's Xinjiang Uyghur Autonomous Region.*

Bovingdon, Gardner, and Nebijan Tursun. 2004. "Contested Histories." In *Xinjiang: China's Muslim Frontier*, ed. S. F. Starr. Armonk: M.E. Sharpe.

Brubaker, Rogers. 1996. *Nationalism Reframed: Nationhood and the National Question in the New Europe.* Cambridge: Cambridge University Press.

Bulag, Uradyn Erden. 2000. "Ethnic Resistance with Socialist Characteristics." In *Chinese Society: Change, Conflict and Resistance*, ed. E. J. Perry and M. Selden. London: Routledge.

———. 2004. "Inner Mongolia: The Dialectics of Colonization and Ethnicity Building." In *Governing China's Multiethnic Frontiers*, ed. M. Rossabi. Seattle: University of Washington Press.

Chen, Kathy. 1994a. "Muslims in China Hate Beijing a Bit Less—Recent Economic Gains Temper Calls for Revolt." *Wall Street Journal*, Oct. 21, A10.

———. 1994b. "Rags to Riches Story: How Rebiya Kader Made Her Fortune." *Wall Street Journal*, Sept. 21, A1, A6.

Cheung Po-ling. 1992. "'More Autonomy' for Xinjiang to Resist Separatism." *The Standard*, April 1, A5.

Connor, Walker. 1984. *The National Question in Marxist-Leninist Theory and Strategy.* Princeton: Princeton University Press.

Cornell, Svante E. 2002. "Autonomy as a Source of Conflict: Caucasian Conflicts in Theoretical Perspective." *World Politics* 54: 245–76.

Dautcher, Jay Todd. 2000. "Reading Out-of-Print: Popular Culture and Protest on China's Western Frontier." In *China Beyond the Headlines*, ed. T. B. Weston and L. M. Jensen. Lanham: Rowman and Littlefield.

Dillon, Michael. 2002. *Uyghur language and culture under threat in Xinjiang* [Central Asia-Caucasus Analyst]. August 14, accessed online at http://coranet.radicalparty.org/pressreview/print.php?func=detail&par=2862, on January 12, 2004.

———. 2004. *Xinjiang—China's Muslim Far Northwest, Durham East Asia Series.* London: RoutledgeCurzon.

Dreyer, June Teufel. 1976. *China's Forty Millions: Minority Nationalities and National Integration in the People's Republic of China.* Cambridge: Harvard University Press.

———. 1994. "The PLA and Regionalism in Xinjiang." *The Pacific Review* 7 (1): 41–56.

Du Wenzhong. 2002. "Zizhi yu gongzhi: dui Xifang gudian minzu zhengzhi lilun de xianzheng fansi" (Autonomy and collective rule: a constitutionalist reflection on classic Western *minzu* political theory). *Minzu yanjiu* (6): 1–8.

Esposito, Bruce J. 1974. "China's West in the 20th Century." *Military Review* 54(1): 64–75.

Fletcher, Joseph. 1978. "The heyday of the Ch'ing order in Mongolia, Sinkiang and Tibet." In *The Cambridge History of China, Vol. 10: Late Ch'ing, 1800-1911, Part I*, ed. J. K. Fairbank. Cambridge: Cambridge University Press.

Forbes, Andrew W. D. 1986. *Warlords and Muslims in Chinese Central Asia: A political history of Republican Sinkiang* 1911-1949. Cambridge: Cambridge University Press.

Forney, Matthew. 2002. *Man of Constant Sorrow: One Uighur Makes Music for the Masses* Timeasia.com, March 25, accessed online at www.time.com/time/asia/features/xinjiang/culture.html, on April 8, 2002.

Ghalip Isma'il. 1996. *Aptonomiyä nizami we uning alahidiliki. Millätlär Ittipaqi* (*Minzu* unity - Uyghur edition) (4): 28–30.

Gilley, Bruce. 2001. "Uighurs Need Not Apply." *Far Eastern Economic Review*, 23 August, 26.

Gladney, Dru. 1990. "The Ethnogenesis of the Uighur." *Central Asian Survey* 9(1): 1–28.

———. 1991. *Muslim Chinese: Ethnic Nationalism in the People's Republic.* Cambridge: Harvard University Press.

Gladney, Dru C. 1998. "Internal Colonialism and the Uyghur Nationality: Chinese Nationalism and Its Subaltern Subjects." *Cahiers d'études sur la Méditeranée orientale et le monde turco-iranien* 25: 47–63.

———. 2002. "Xinjiang: China's Future West Bank?" *Current History*: 267–70.

———. 2004. "Responses to Chinese Rule: Patterns of Occupation and Opposition." In *Xinjiang: China's Muslim Borderland*, ed. S. F. Starr. Armonk: M. E. Sharpe.

Gleason, Gregory. 1990. *Federalism and Nationalism: The Struggle for Republican Rights in the USSR.* Boulder: Westview.

Goldstein, Melvyn C. 1997. *The Snow Lion and the Dragon: China, Tibet, and the Dalai Lama.* Berkeley: University of California Press.

Gong Yong. 1997. *Qianlun feifa zongjiao huodong dui Xinjiang shehui zhengzhi wending de weihaixing* (A brief discussion of the nature of the threat of illegal activity to Xinjiang's social and political stability). Ürümci: Xinjiang University. Conference paper.

Guo Zhengli. 1992. *Zhongguo tese de minzu quyu zizhi lilun yu shijian* (The theory and practice of *minzu* regional autonomy [with] Chinese characteristics). Urumqi: Xinjiang Daxue Chubanshe.

Guowuyuan xinwen bangongshi. 2002. "'Dong Tu' kongbu shili nantuo zuize" (The "ET" Terrorist Forces Cannot Escape Their Crimes). Beijing.

Gurr, Ted Robert. 1993. *Minorities at Risk: A Global View of Ethnopolitical Conflicts.* Washington: United States Institute of Peace Press.

Hagt, Eric. 2003. "China's Water Policies: Implications for Xinjiang and Kazakhstan." *Central Asia-Caucasus Analyst.*

Hannum, Emily, and Yu Xie. 1998. "Ethnic Stratification in Northwest China: Occupational Differences between Han Chinese and National Minorities in Xinjiang, 1982-1990." *Demography* 35(3): 323–33.

Hannum, Hurst, and Richard B. Lillich. 1980. "The Concept of Autonomy in International Law." *American Journal of International Law* 74(4): 858–89.

Hansen, Mette Halskov. 1999. *Lessons in Being Chinese: Minority Education and Ethnic Identity in Southwest China.* Seattle: University of Washington Press.

Harris, Lillian Craig. 1993. "Xinjiang, Central Asia and the Implications for China's Policy in the Islamic World." *China Quarterly* 133: 111–29.

He Gang, and Shi Weimin. 1994. *Monan qing: Nei Menggu shengchan jianshe bingtuan xiezhen* (The situation south of the Gobi: the true story of the Inner Mongolia PCC). Beijing: Falü chubanshe.

Heberer, Thomas. 1989. *China and Its National Minorities: Autonomy or Assimilation?* Armonk: M.E. Sharpe.

Hechter, Michael. 1975. *Internal Colonialism: The Celtic Fringe in British National Development,* 1536-1966. Berkeley: University of California.

Huang Guangxue. 2001. "Dang de san dai lingdao jiti guanyu minzu gongzuo de zhidao sixiang" (The guiding principles concerning *minzu* work held by the Party's three generations of leadership groups). *Zhongguo minzu (China Ethnicity)* (7).

Ji Ping. 1990. "Frontier Migration and Ethnic Assimilation: A Case of Xinjiang Uygur Autonomous Region." Ph.D. dissertation, Sociology, Brown University, Providence.

Kapstein, Matthew. 2004. "A Thorn in the Dragon's Side: Tibetan Buddhist Culture in China." In *Governing China's Multiethnic Frontiers,* ed. by M. Rossabi. Seattle: University of Washington Press.

Kashi diwei xuanchuan bu. 1995. "Fandui minzu fenlie, weihu zuguo tongyi, weihu minzu tuanjie, weihu shehui wending (xuanchuan jiaoyu cailiao)" (Oppose *minzu* separatism, protect the unification of the motherland, protect *minzu* unity, protect social stability (propaganda education materials)). Kashgar: (internal circulation).

Kaup, Katherine Palmer. 2000. *Creating the Zhuang: Ethnic Politics in China.* Boulder: Lynne Rienner.

Kuran, Timur. 1992. "Now Out of Never: The Element of Surprise in the East European Revolution of 1989." In *Liberalization and Democratization: Change in the Soviet Union and Eastern Europe,* ed. N. Bermeo. Baltimore: Johns Hopkins University Press.

Laird, Thomas. 2002. *Into Tibet: The CIA's First Atomic Spy and His Secret Expedition to Lhasa.* New York: Grove Press.

Laitin, David D. 1991. "The National Uprising in the Soviet Union." *World Politics* 44 (October): 139–77.

Lawrence, Susan V. 2000. "Where Beijing Fears Kosovo." *Far Eastern Economic Review*, September 7.

Li Ailing, Li Hongxun, Ma Yan, and Zhang Guolin. 1992. *Ate'izm terbiyisi toghrisida qisqice oqushluq* (A concise text concerning education in atheism). Translated by T. Sadiq. Ürümci: Shinjang yashlar osmurler neshriyati.

Li Weihan. 1982. *Tongyi zhanxian wenti yu minzu wenti* (United front problems and *minzu* problems). Beijing: Renmin chubanshe.

Lim, Louisa. 2003. "China's high-stakes war on terror," BBC News online, November 3, 2003, accessed online at http://news.bbc.co.uk/go/pr/fr/-/1/hi/world/asia-pacific/3223939.stm, on November 11, 2003.

Lipman, Jonathan. 1997. *Familiar Strangers: a History of Muslims in Northwest China*. Seattle: University of Washington Press.

Liu Zhongkang. 1990. "Bo 'Guoqu Malie zhuyi ya zongjiao, xianzai zongjiao yao yadao Malie zhuyi' de miulun" (A refutation of the preposterous idea that "In the past Marxism-Leninism suppressed religion; now religion will overwhelm Marxism-Leninism"). *Xinjiang shehui kexue yanjiu* (special issue): 50–55.

———. 1996. "Feifa zongjiao huodong ji qi weihai" (Illegal religious activities and what they threaten). *Xinjiang shehui jingji* (5): 66–69.

Luo Yingfu. 1992. *Zongjiao wenti jianlun* (A brief discussion of the religious question). Wulumuqi: Xinjiang renmin chubanshe.

Ma Dazheng. 2003. "Guojia liyi gaoyu yiqie—Xinjiang wending wenti de guancha yu sikao"(The national interest above all else—analysis of and reflections on the problem of stability in Xinjiang), ed. Zhongguo shehui kexueyuan Xinjiang fazhan yanjiu zhongxin, *Xinjiang yanjiu congshu*. Ürümci: Xinjiang renmin chubanshe.

Mackerras, Colin. 1994. *China's Minorities: Integration and Modernization in the Twentieth Century*. Oxford: Oxford University Press.

Mao Yongfu, and Li Ling. 1996. "Nanjiang san dizhou shehui jingji fazhan de shehuixue sikao" (Sociological reflections on socioeconomic development in three regions of southern Xinjiang). In *Xinjiang minzu guanxi yanjiu* (Research on *minzu* relations in Xinjiang), ed. Yin Zhuguang and Mao Yongfu. Urumchi: Xinjiang Renmin Chubanshe.

McMillen, Donald. 1981. "Xinjiang and the Production and Construction Corps: A Han Organization in a non-Han Region." *Australian Journal of Chinese Affairs* (6): 65–96.

———. 1984. "Xinjiang and Wang Enmao: New Directions in Power, Policy, and Integration?" *China Quarterly* (99): 569–93.

McMillen, Donald H. 1979. *Chinese Communist Power and Policy in Xinjiang, 1949–77*. Boulder: Westview Press.

Millward, James A. 2000. "Historical Perspectives on Contemporary Xinjiang." *Inner Asia* 2(2): 121–35.

Millward, James A., and Nabijan Tursun. 2004. "Political History and Strategies of Control, 1884–1978." In *Xinjiang: China's Muslim Borderland*, ed. S. F. Starr. Armonk: M. E. Sharpe.

Moneyhon, Matthew. 2002. "Controlling Xinjiang: Autonomy on China's New Frontier." *Asia-Pacific Law & Policy Journal* 3(1): 120–52.

Moseley, George. 1965. "China's Fresh Approach to the National Minority Question." *China Quarterly* (24): 14–27.

Pan Zhiping, ed. 1999. *Minzu zijue haishi minzu fenlie* (*Minzu* self-determination or *minzu* splitting). Ürümci: Xinjiang Renmin Chubanshe.

Pei Minxin. 2002. "Self-Administration and Local Autonomy: Reconciling Conflicting Interests in China." In *The Self-Determination of Peoples: Community, Nation, and State in an Interdependent World*, ed. W. Danspeckgruber. Boulder: Lynne Rienner.

Qiu Yuanyao, ed. 1994. *Kua shijide Zhongguo renkou: Xinjiang juan* (China's population across the millennial divide: Xinjiang volume). Beijing: Zhongguo tongji chubanshe.

Roeder, Philip G. 1991. "Soviet Federalism and Ethnic Mobilization." *World Politics* 43: 196–232.

Rossabi, Morris, ed. 2004. *Governing China's Multiethnic Frontiers.* Seattle: University of Washington Press.

Rudelson, Justin, and William Jankowiak. 2004. "Acculturation and Resistance: Xinjiang Identities in Flux." In *Xinjiang: China's Muslim Borderland*, ed. by S. F. Starr. Armonk: M. E. Sharpe.

Rudelson, Justin Jon. 1997. *Oasis Identities: Uyghur Nationalism Along China's Silk Road.* New York: Columbia University Press.

Sautman, Barry. 1998. "Preferential Policies for Ethnic Minorities in China: The Case of Xinjiang." *Nationalism and Ethnic Politics* 4(1&2): 86–118.

———. 1999. "Ethnic Law and Minority Rights in China." *Law and Policy* 21(3): 283–314.

———. 2000. "Is Xinjiang an Internal Colony?" *Inner Asia* 2(2): 239–71.

Scott, James C. 1985. *Weapons of the Weak: Everyday Forms of Peasant Resistance.* New Haven: Yale University Press.

———. 1990. *Domination and the Arts of Resistance: Hidden Transcripts.* New Haven: Yale University Press.

Seymour, James D. 2000. "Xinjiang's Production and Construction Corps, and the Sinification of Eastern Turkestan." *Inner Asia* 2(2): 171–93.

Shakya, Tsering W. 1999. *The Dragon in the Land of Snows: A History of Modern Tibet since 1947.* New York: Columbia University Press.

Shichor, Yitzhak. 2001. "Virtual Transnationalism: Uygur Communities in Europe and the Quest for Eastern Turkestan Independence." Florence: European University Institute.

———. 2004. "The Great Wall of Steel: Military and Strategy in Xinjiang." In *Xinjiang: China's Muslim Borderland*, ed. S. F. Starr. Armonk: M. E. Sharpe.

Smith, Joanne. 2000. "Four Generations of Uyghurs: The Shift towards Ethno-political Ideologies among Xinjiang's Youth." *Inner Asia* 2(2): 195–224.

———. Forthcoming. "Barren Chickens, Stray Dogs, Fake Immortals and Thieves: Coloniser and Collaborator in Popular Uyghur Song and the Quest for National Unity." In *Music, National Identity, and the Politics of Location: Between the Global and the Local*, ed. I. Biddle and V. Knights. Aldershot: Ashgate.

Stein, Justin J. 2003. "Taking the Deliberative Turn in China: International Law, Minority Rights, and the Case of Xinjiang." *Journal of Public and International Affairs* 14: 1–25.

Tanner, Harold M. 1999. *Strike Hard! Anti-Crime Campaigns and Chinese Criminal Justice 1979-1985.* Ithaca: Cornell East Asia Program.

Toops, Stanley. 1992. "Recent Uygur Leaders in Xinjiang." *Central Asian Survey* 11(2): 77–99.

———. 2004a. "The Demography of Xinjiang." In *Xinjiang: China's Muslim Borderland*, ed. S. F. Starr. Armonk: M.E. Sharpe.

———. 2004b. "The Ecology of Xinjiang: A Focus on Water." In *Xinjiang: China's Muslim Borderland*, ed. S. F. Starr. Armonk: M. E. Sharpe.

Walder, Andrew. 1986. *Communist Neo-Traditionalism: Work and Authority in Chinese Industry.* Berkeley: University of California Press.

Wang, David. 1998. "Han Migration and Social Changes in Xinjiang." *Issues and Studies* 34(7): 33–61.

———. 1999. *Under the Soviet Shadow: The Yining Incident, Ethnic Conflicts and International Rivalry in Xinjiang, 1944-49.* Hong Kong: Chinese University Press.

Wang Shuanqian, ed. 1999. *Zou xiang 21 shiji de Xinjiang-zhengzhi juan* (Xinjiang heading into the 21st century-volume on politics). Ürümci: Xinjiang Renmin Chubanshe.

Weimer, Calla. 2004. "The Economy of Xinjiang." *In Xinjiang: China's Muslim Borderland*, ed. S. F. Starr. Armonk: M. E. Sharpe.

Wen Hui, Wang Peng, and Li Bengang, eds. 1992. *Dangdai xin ciyu da cidian* (The big dictionary of contemporary neologisms). Dalian: Dalian chubanshe.

Xinjiang Weiwuer Zizhiqu Tongjiju, ed. 1995. *Xinjiang Tongji Nianjian* (Xinjiang Statistical Yearbook) 1995. Beijing: Zhongguo Tongji Chubanshe.

Xu Xifa. 1995. *Zhongguo shaoshu minzu jihua shengyu* gailun (An introduction to family planning for China's minority *minzu*). Urumqi: Xinjiang renmin chubanshe.

Xu Yuqi, ed. 1999. *Xinjiang fandui minzu fenlie zhuyi douzheng shihua* (Narrative history of Xinjiang's struggle against *minzu* splittism). Ürümci: Xinjiang renmin chubanshe.

"*XUAR gaikuang*" bianxiezu, ed. 1985. *Xinjiang Weiwu'er Zizhiqu gaikuang* (An overview of conditions in the XUAR). Urumqi: Xinjiang Renmin Chubanshe.

XUAR local gazetteer editorial committee, ed. 1995. *Xinjiang Nianjian* (Xinjiang Yearbook) *1995.* Urumqi: Xinjiang Renmin Chubanshe.

XUAR Party Committee Propaganda Bureau, ed. 1997. *Minzu tuanjie jiaoyu duben* (A reader on education in *minzu* unity). Ürümci: Xinjiang Qingshaonian Chubanshe.

XueYu (pseudonym: Snowy Regions). 2003. "Qianyi Xinjiang de fenlie zhuyi wenti de lishi he jintian zhengfu de duice" (A simple view of the history of and current government's policies for handling the problem of splittism in Xinjiang), Xuhuan junshi tiankong, accessed online at www.war-sky.com/cgi-bin/forums.cgi?forum=70&topic=4813, on November 4, 2003.

Yang Faren. 2000. *Deng Xiaoping minzu lilun ji qi zai Xinjiang de shijian* (Deng Xiaoping's *minzu* theory and its practical application in Xinjiang). Ürümci: Xinjiang Renmin Chubanshe.

Yang Zhenhua, ed. 1997. *Shichang jingji yu tunken shubian* (Market economics and reclaiming land to garrison the frontiers). Ürümci: Xinjiang Renmin Chubanshe.

Yee, Herbert S. 2003. "Ethnic Relations in Xinjiang: A Survey of Uygur-Han Relations in Urumqi." *Journal of Contemporary China* 12(36): 431–52.

Yin Zhuguang, and Mao Yongfu, eds. 1996. *Xinjiang minzu guanxi yanjiu* (Research on *minzu* relations in Xinjiang). Urumchi: Xinjiang Renmin Chubanshe.

Yu Xingzhong. 2004. *From State Leadership to State Responsibility—Comments on the New PRC Law on Regional Autonomy of Ethnic Minorities* [Working paper]. Chinese University, accessed online at www.cuhk.edu.hk/gpa/xzyu/work1.htm, on May 2, 2004.

Zhang Erju, ed. 1988. *Zhongguo minzu quyu zizhi de lilun he shijian* (The theory and practice of *minzu* regional autonomy in China). Beijing: Zhongguo Shehui Chubanshe.

Zhang Yuxi. 1993. "Xinjiang jiefang yilai fandui minzu fenliezhuyi de douzheng ji qi lishi jingyan" (The struggle and historical experience of opposition to *minzu* separatism in Xinjiang since liberation). In *Fan yisilan zhuyi, fan tujue zhuyi yanjiu* (Research on Pan-Islamism and Pan-Turkism), ed. Yang Faren. Urumqi: (neibu).

Zhou Enlai. 1980 (1957). "Guanyu woguo minzu zhengce de jige wenti" (A few problems of our country's *minzu* policies). *Minzu yanjiu* (1): 1–11.

Zhu Lun. 2002. "Lun minzu gongzhi de lilun jichu yu jiben yuanli" (A discussion of the theoretical basis and basic tenets of *minzu* collective rule). *Minzu yanjiu* (2): 1–9.

Zhu Peimin. 2000. *20shiji Xinjiang shi yanjiu* (Research on the history of Xinjiang in the 20th century). Ürümci: Xinjiang renmin.

Zongjiao yanjiusuo Yisilanjiao diaocha zu. 1983. "Xinjiang Kashi, Hetian Yisilanjiao qingkuang diaocha" (An investigation into the situation of Islam in Xinjiang's Kashgar and Hotän). *Xinjiang shehui kexue yanjiu* 126: 16–42.

Background of the Xinjiang Conflict

The Xinjiang Uyghur Autonomous Region, as it is officially known to the Chinese (Uyghur nationalists call it "East Turkistan" or "Uyghuristan"), is a vast region in the northwestern corner of the People's Republic of China. Occupying one-sixth the total area of China, it holds only a fraction more than 1 percent of China's population, some 18 million. Xinjiang possesses rich deposits of oil, natural gas, and nonferrous metals. Chinese officials value it as a space to absorb migrants, a source of resources crucial to economic development, and a link to Central Asia. They desperately want to maintain hold of Xinjiang, fearing its loss would incite the CCP's collapse and possibly the secession of Taiwan and Tibet.

While a succession of Qing (1644–1911), Republican (1912–49), and Communist governments all laid formal claim to the territory and inhabitants of what is today Xinjiang, locals have resented and resisted each assertion of authority. Official Chinese sources claim that Xinjiang and the Uyghurs have been part of China "since ancient times," dating incorporation to the first century B.C. Yet only in the mid-eighteenth century was the whole of the region conquered militarily from the east, and then by the Manchu Qing empire. Qing rulers made the region a province only in the late nineteenth century, fearing its loss due to foreign incursions or internal rebellion. Between 1867 and 1877, for instance, Qing rulers lost control of the region when Yaqub Beg established an independent kingdom that achieved diplomatic relations with Turkey and Britain. Opposition to rule from Beijing (and for a time Nanjing) continued after the collapse of the Manchu empire and the founding of the Republic of China in 1912: Turki leaders twice established independent states of "East Turkistan"— once briefly in the southwest from 1933 to 1934 and again more successfully in the three northwestern prefectures of Xinjiang from 1944 to 1949.

Nor has the Chinese Communist Party been immune from challenges in the region. Though the party killed, imprisoned, or co-opted nearly all advocates of independence soon after taking power in 1949, Uyghur aspirations to independence did not disappear. Uyghurs within Xinjiang organized a number of opposition parties in the first postrevolutionary decade (nearly all of them quickly squelched by the party-state). Uyghur emigrés in Soviet Central Asia and Turkey continued to harbor the dream of establishing an independent Uyghur state. While the high socialist era in Xinjiang (1958–76) witnessed little secessionist violence, Chinese officials claim to have exposed several underground organizations. In 1962 tens of thousands of Uyghurs and Kazakhs rioted in the northwest city of Ghulja, and more than 60,000 fled Xinjiang for the Soviet Union. Uyghur nationalism found renewed public expression in the Reform Era (1978–), and participants in several demonstrations in the late 1980s called for independence. Peaceful demonstrations disappeared in the wake of the Tian'anmen crackdown in 1989. Since 1990 a series of violent episodes in Xinjiang has drawn international attention. The Baren Uprising in April 1990, in which several dozen Uyghurs attacked the regional government and police, was the most violent clash. Bus bombings in Urumchi in 1992 and 1997 left over ten dead and led some to label Uyghur separatists terrorists. A peaceful demonstration in Hotan in 1995, and a much larger one in Ghulja in 1997, turned violent after police attacked the demonstrators. A spate of political assassinations of regional officials and religious clerics has created a sense of uncertainty in parts of the region. Nevertheless, since 1949 there has not been a "hot conflict" in Xinjiang like those in Palestine, Chechnya, Aceh, or Mindanao. Underground Uyghur organizations in Xinjiang are all but unheard of, and there are no independent militias. Given the relative scarcity of collective violence, no international agent has explicitly called for intervention or mediation.

The Uyghur Autonomous Region contains several non-Uyghur majority prefectures. These are: Kizilsu (Kirghiz autonomous prefecture), Altay, Tarbaghatay, and Ili (Kazakh autonomous prefectures), Bortala and Bayangol (Mongol autonomous prefectures), and Changji (Hui autonomous prefecture).

Note: Map boundaries and locations are approximate. Geographic features and their names do not imply official endorsement or recognition by the UN.

© 2004 by East-West Center
www.eastwestcenter.org

Project Information

The Dynamics and Management of Internal Conflicts in Asia
Project Rationale, Purpose and Outline

Project Director: Muthiah Alagappa
Principal Researchers: Edward Aspinall (Aceh)
                      Danilyn Rutherford (Papua)
                      Christopher Collier (southern Philippines)
                      Gardner Bovingdon (Xinjiang)
                      Elliot Sperling (Tibet)

Rationale

Internal conflicts have been a prominent feature of the Asian political landscape since 1945. Asia has witnessed numerous civil wars, armed insurgencies, coups d'etat, regional rebellions, and revolutions. Many have been protracted; several have far reaching domestic and international consequences. The civil war in Pakistan led to the break up of that country in 1971; separatist struggles challenge the political and territorial integrity of China, India, Indonesia, Burma, the Philippines, Thailand, and Sri Lanka; political uprisings in Thailand (1973 and 1991), the Philippines (1986), South Korea (1986), Taiwan, Bangladesh (1991), and Indonesia (1998) resulted in dramatic political change in those countries; although the political uprisings in Burma (1988) and China (1989) were suppressed, the political systems in these countries as well as in Vietnam continue to confront problems of political legitimacy that could become acute; and radical Islam poses serious challenges to stability in Pakistan, Indonesia, Malaysia, and India. In all, millions of people have been killed in the internal conflicts, and tens of millions have been displaced. And the involvement of external powers in a competitive manner (especially during the Cold War) in several of these conflicts had negative consequences for domestic and regional security.

Internal conflicts in Asia (as elsewhere) can be traced to three issues—national identity, political legitimacy (the title to rule), and distributive justice—that are often interconnected. With the bankruptcy of the socialist model and the transitions to democracy in several countries, the number of internal conflicts over the legitimacy of political system has declined in Asia. However, political legitimacy of certain governments continues to be contested from time to time and the legitimacy of the remaining communist and authoritarian systems is likely to confront challenges in due course. The project deals with internal conflicts arising from the process of constructing national identity with specific focus on conflicts rooted in the relationship of minority communities to the nation-state. Here too many Asian states have made considerable progress in constructing national communities but several states including some major ones still confront serious problems that have degenerated into violent conflict. By affecting the political and territorial integrity of the state as well as the physical, cultural, economic, and political security of individuals and groups, these conflicts have great potential to affect domestic and international stability.

Purpose

The project investigates the dynamics and management of five key internal conflicts in Asia—Aceh and Papua in Indonesia, the Moro conflict in the southern Philippines, and the conflicts pertaining to Tibet and Xinjiang in China. Specifically it investigates the following:

1. Why (on what basis), how (in what form), and when does group differentiation and political consciousness emerge?
2. What are the specific issues of contention in such conflicts? Are these of the instrumental or cognitive type? If both, what is the relationship between them? Have the issues of contention altered over time? Are the conflicts likely to undergo further redefinition?
3. When, why, and under what circumstances can such contentions lead to violent conflict? Under what circumstances have they not led to violent conflict?
4. How can the conflicts be managed, settled, and eventually resolved? What are policy choices? Do options such as national self-determination, autonomy, federalism, electoral design, and consociationalism exhaust the list of choices available to meet the aspirations of minority communities? Are there innovative ways of thinking about identity and sovereignty that can meet the aspirations of the minority communities without creating new sovereign nation-states?
5. What is the role of the regional and international communities in the protection of minority communities?
6. How and when does a policy choice become relevant?

Design

A study group has been organized for each of the five conflicts investigated in the study. With a principal researcher each, the study groups comprise practitioners and scholars from the respective Asian countries including the region or province that is the focus of the conflict, the United States, and Australia. For composition of study groups please see the participants list.

All five study-groups met jointly for the first time in Washington, D.C. from September 29 through October 3, 2002. Over a period of four days, participants engaged in intensive discussion of a wide range of issues pertaining to the five conflicts investigated in the project. In addition to identifying key issues for research and publication, the meeting facilitated the development of cross country perspectives and interaction among scholars who had not previously worked together. Based on discussion at the meeting five research monograph length studies (one per conflict) and twenty policy papers (four per conflict) were commissioned.

Study groups met separately for the second meeting. The Aceh and Papua study group meetings were held in Bali on June 16–17, the southern Philippines study group met in Manila on June 23, and the Tibet and Xinjiang study groups were held in Honolulu on August 20–22, 2003. The third meeting of all study groups was held in Washington, D.C. from February 28 to March 2, 2004. These meetings reviewed recent developments relating to the conflicts, critically reviewed the first drafts of the policy papers prepared for the project, reviewed the book proposals by the principal researchers, and identified new topics for research.

Publications

The project will result in five research monographs (book length studies) and about twenty policy papers.

Research Monographs. To be authored by the principal researchers, these monographs present a book-length study of the key issues pertaining to each of the five conflicts. Subject to satisfactory peer review, the monographs will appear in the East-West Center Washington series *Asian Security*, and the East-West Center series *Contemporary Issues in the Asia Pacific*, both published by the Stanford University Press.

Policy Papers. The policy papers provide a detailed study of particular aspects of each conflict. Subject to satisfactory peer review, these 10,000- to 25,000-word essays will be published in the East-West Center Washington *Policy Studies* series, and be circulated widely to key personnel and institutions in the policy and intellectual communities and the media in the respective Asian countries, United States, and other relevant countries.

Public Forums

To engage the informed public and to disseminate the findings of the project to a wide audience, public forums have been organized in conjunction with study group meetings.

Two public forums were organized in Washington, D.C. in conjunction with the first study group meeting. The first forum, cosponsored by the United States-Indonesia Society, discussed the Aceh and Papua conflicts. The second forum, cosponsored by the United States Institute of Peace, the Asia Program of the Woodrow Wilson International Center, and the Sigur Center of the George Washington University, discussed the Tibet and Xinjiang conflicts.

Public forums were also organized in Jakarta and Manila in conjunction with the second study group meetings. The Jakarta public forum on Aceh and Papua, cosponsored by the Center for Strategic and International Studies in Jakarta, and the southern Philippines public forum cosponsored by the Policy Center of the Asian Institute of Management attracted key persons from government, media, think tanks, activist groups, diplomatic community, and the public.

In conjunction with the third study group meetings, also held in Washington, D.C., three public forums were offered. The first forum, cosponsored by the United States-Indonesia Society, addressed the conflicts in Aceh and Papua. The second forum, cosponsored by the Sigur Center of The George Washington University, discussed the conflicts in Tibet and Xinjiang. A third forum was held to discuss the conflict in the southern Philippines. This forum was cosponsored by the United States Institute of Peace.

Funding Support

This project is supported with a generous grant from the Carnegie Corporation of New York.

Project Director
Muthiah Alagappa
East-West Center Washington

Aceh Study Group

Edward Aspinall
University of Sydney
Principal Researcher

Saifuddin Bantasyam
Human Rights Forum, Banda Aceh

Harold Crouch
Australian National University

Ahmad Humam Hamid
Care Human Rights, Banda Aceh

Bob Hadiwinata
University of Parahyangan, Indonesia

Konrad Huber
USAID, Washington, D.C.

Sidney Jones
International Crisis Group, Jakarta

T. Mulya Lubis
Lubis, Santosa and Maulana, Jakarta

Marcus Meitzner
USAID, Jakarta

Kelli Muddell
International Center for Transitional
    Justice, New York

Michael Ross
University of California, Los Angeles

Kirsten E. Schulze
London School of Economics

Rizal Sukma
CSIS, Jakarta

Paul Van Zyl
International Center for Transitional
    Justice, New York

Agus Widjojo
Former Chief of Staff for Territorial
    Affairs, Government of Indonesia

Sastrohandoyo Wiryono
Chief Negotiator for the Government
    of Indonesia in the peace talks with
    the Free Aceh Movement

Daniel Ziv
USAID, Jakarta

Papua Study Group

Danilyn Rutherford
University of Chicago
Principal Researcher

Ikrar Nusa Bhakti
Indonesian Institute of Sciences
    (LIPI), Jakarta

Richard Chauvel
Victoria University, Melbourne

Benny Giay
The Institute for Human Rights Study
    and Advocacy, Jayapura

Barbara Harvey
Former Deputy Chief of Mission for
    the U.S. Embassy in Indonesia

Rodd McGibbon
USAID, Jakarta

Papua Study Group continued

Octavianus Mote
Yale University

Samsu Rizal Panggabean
Gadjah Mada University, Yogyakarta

John Rumbiak
ELS-HAM, Jayapura

Barnabas Suebu
Former Governor of Irian Jaya

Agus Sumule
Universitas Negeri Papua, Amban

Southern Philippines Study Group

Christopher Collier
Australian National University
Principal Researcher

Robert F. Barnes
USAID, Philippines

Noemi Bautista
USAID, Philippines

Saturnino M. Borras, Jr.
Institute of Social Studies, The Hague

Jesus Dureza
Presidential Assistant for Mindanao,
Philippines

Alma Evangelista
United Nations Development
Programme, Manila

Eric Gutierrez
WaterAid, United Kingdom

Carolina Hernandez
Institute for Strategic and
Development Studies, Manila

Abraham S. Iribani
Assistant Secretary, Department of the
Interior and Local Government
Government of the Philippines,
Manila

Mary Judd
The World Bank, Philippines

Macapado Muslim
Mindanao State University
Fatima, General Santos City

Amina Rasul-Bernardo
Asian Institute of Management,
Manila

Steven Rood
The Asia Foundation, Philippines

David Timberman
USAID, Washington, D.C.

Michael Yates
USAID, Philippines

Tibet Study Group

Elliot Sperling
Indiana University, Bloomington
Principal Researcher

Allen Carlson
Cornell University

Tibet Study Group continued

Shulong Chu
Tsinghua University, Beijing

Yongbin Du
Chinese Center for Tibet Studies,
Beijing

Mark D. Koehler
U.S. Department of State

Carole McGranahan
University of Colorado at Boulder

Warren W. Smith, Jr.
Radio Free Asia

Tashi Rabgey
Harvard University

Tseten Wangchuk
Voice of America

Xinjiang Study Group

Gardner Bovingdon
Indiana University, Bloomington
Principal Researcher

Jay Dautcher
University of Pennsylvania

Arienne Dwyer
University of Kansas

Talant Mawkanuli
Indiana University, Bloomington

James Millward
Georgetown University

Susan Shirk
University of California, San Diego

Stan Toops
Miami University

Nury Turkel
American University

Nabijan Tursun
Radio Free Asia

Shengmin Yang
Central University for Nationalities,
Beijing

Other Participants

Allen Choate
Asia Foundation, Hong Kong

Chester Crocker
Georgetown University

Stephen Del Rosso, Jr.
Carnegie Corporation of New York

Pauline Kerr
Australian National University

Federico M. Macaranas
Asian Institute of Management,
Manila

Christopher McNally
East-West Center

Charles Morrison
East-West Center

Holly Morrow
U.S. Department of State

Hadi Soesastro
CSIS, Jakarta

Sheila Smith
East-West Center

Arun Swamy
East-West Center

Barbara Walter
University of California, San Diego

List of Reviewers 2003–04

The East-West Center Washington would like to acknowledge the following, who have offered reviews of manuscripts for *Policy Studies*.

Pamela Aall
United States Institute of Peace

Patricio Nunes Abinales
Kyoto University

Muthiah Alagappa
East-West Center Washington

Dewi Fortuna Anwar
Indonesian Institute of Sciences (LIPI)

Edward Aspinall
The University of Sydney

Robert Barnett
Columbia University

Gardner Bovingdon
Indiana University, Bloomington

Leslie Butt
University of Victoria

Allen Carlson
Cornell University

Harold Crouch
Australian National University

Jay Dautcher
University of Pennsylvania

June Teufel Dreyer
University of Miami

Sumit Ganguly
Indiana University, Bloomington

Brigham Golden
Columbia University

Reuel Hanks
Oklahoma State University

Eva-Lotta Hedman
University of Oxford

Paul Hutchcroft
University of Wisconsin

Sidney Jones
International Crisis Group

Stephanie Lawson
University of East Anglia

David Leheny
University of Wisconsin, Madison

Tashi Rabgey
Harvard University

Geoffrey Robinson
University of California-
Los Angeles

Michael Ross
University of California, Los Angeles

Danilyn Rutherford
University of Chicago

Yitzhak Shichor
The Hebrew University of Jerusalem

Timothy Sisk
University of Denver

Anthony Smith
Asia Pacific Center for Security
Studies, Honolulu

Warren W. Smith
Radio Free Asia

Elliot Sperling
Indiana University, Bloomington

Geoffrey White
East-West Center

Barbara Walter
University of California, San Diego

Policy Studies

Previous Publications

Policy Studies 1
The Aceh Peace Process:
Why it Failed

> Dr. Edward Aspinall, University of
> Sydney
> Dr. Harold Crouch, Australian National
> University

Policy Studies 2
The Free Aceh Movement (GAM):
Anatomy of a Separatist Organization

> Dr. Kirsten E. Schulze, London School
> of Economics

Policy Studies 3
Security Operations in Aceh:
Goals, Consequences, and Lessons

> Dr. Rizal Sukma, Centre for Strategic
> and International Studies, Jakarta

Policy Studies 4
Beijing's Tibet Policy:
Securing Sovereignty and Legitimacy

> Dr. Allen Carlson, Cornell University

Policy Studies 5
The Papua Conflict:
Jakarta's Perceptions and Policies

> Dr. Richard Chauvel, Victoria
> University, Melbourne
> Dr. Ikrar Nusa Bhakti, Indonesian
> Institute of Sciences, Jakarta

Policy Studies 6
Violent Separatism in Xinjiang:
A Critical Assessment

> Dr. James Millward, Georgetown
> University

Policy Studies 7
The Tibet-China Conflict:
History and Polemics

> Dr. Elliot Sperling, Indiana University,
> Bloomington

Policy Studies 8
The Moro Conflict:
Landlessness and Misdirected State
Policies

> Mr. Eric Guitierrez, WaterAid, U.K.
> Mr. Saturnino Borras, Jr., Institute of
> Social Studies, The Hague

Policy Studies 9
The HDC in Aceh:
Promises and Pitfalls of NGO
Mediation and Implementation

> Mr. Konrad Huber, Council on Foreign
> Relations

Policy Studies 10
Secessionist Challenges in Aceh
and Papua:
Is Special Autonomy the Solution?

> Dr. Rodd McGibbon, USAID, Jakarta

These issues of *Policy Studies* are presently available in print and online.
Online at: www.eastwestcenterwashington.org/publications/

Policy Studies

A Publication of the East-West Center Washington

Editor: Dr. Muthiah Alagappa

The aim of *Policy Studies* is to present scholarly analysis of key contemporary domestic and international political, economic, and strategic issues affecting Asia in a policy relevant manner. Written for the policy community, academics, journalists, and the informed public, the peer-reviewed publications in this series will provide new policy insights and perspectives based on extensive fieldwork and rigorous scholarship.

Each publication in the series presents a 15,000- to 25,000-word investigation of a single topic. Often publications in this series will appear in conjunction with East-West Center research projects; stand-alone investigations of pertinent issues will also appear in the series.

Submissions

Submissions may take the form of a proposal or completed manuscript.

Proposal. A three- to five-page proposal should indicate the issue, problem, or puzzle to be analyzed, its policy significance, the novel perspective to be provided, and date by which the manuscript will be ready. The editor and two relevant experts will review proposals to determine their suitability for the series. The manuscript when completed will be peer-reviewed in line with the double-blind process.

Complete Manuscript. Submission of complete manuscript should be accompanied by a two-page abstract that sets out the issue, problem, or puzzle analyzed, its policy significance, and the novel perspective provided by the paper. The editor and two relevant experts will review the abstract. If considered suitable for the series, the manuscript will be peer-reviewed in line with the double-blind process.

Submissions must be original and not published elsewhere. The East-West Center Washington will have copyright over material published in the series.

A CV indicating relevant qualifications and publications should accompany submissions.

Notes to Contributors

Manuscripts should be typed and double-spaced. Citations should be inserted in the text with notes double-spaced at the end. The manuscript should be accompanied by a completed bibliography. All artwork should be camera ready. Authors should refrain from identifying themselves in their proposals and manuscripts and should follow the *Policy Studies* style sheet, available from the series' editorial office. Submissions should be sent to:

Editor, *Policy Studies*
East-West Center Washington
1819 L Street, NW, Suite 200
Washington, D.C.   20036

Submissions can also be forwarded by e-mail to
publications@eastwestcenterwashington.org

www.ingramcontent.com/pod-product-compliance
Lightning Source LLC
Chambersburg PA
CBHW061037050726

47592CB00004B/1477